Grenadier

Grenadier

The Recollections of an
Officer of the Grenadier Guards
throughout the Great War on the
Western Front

E. R. M. Fryer

LEONAUR

Grenadier: The Recollections of an
Officer of the Grenadier Guards throughout
the Great War on the Western Front
by E. R. M. Fryer

First published under the title
Reminiscences of a Grenadier

Leonaur is an imprint
of Oakpast Ltd

ISBN: 978-1-84677-650-2 (hardcover)
ISBN: 978-1-84677-649-6 (softcover)

http://www.leonaur.com

Publisher's Notes

In the interests of authenticity, the spellings, grammar and place names
used have been retained from the original editions.

The opinions of the authors represent a view of events in which he
was a participant related from his own perspective,
as such the text is relevant as an historical document.

The views expressed in this book are not necessarily
those of the publisher.

Contents

CHAPTER 1

The Early Days

Everyone knows how the war started; if they don't, it is through their own idleness, as books on the subject are legion; I do not propose, therefore, to do more than tell how it started for me and for many more harmless civilians at that time employed in peaceful occupations.

The London Season had just come to its allotted end, a season perhaps more magnificent than any of its forerunners. Everyone had given themselves up to amusement; this, indeed, seemed to be the sole object of existence. Whether people had any foreboding of the misery that was to descend on the world I know not, but I remember often feeling that something vague was going to happen, and that the season of 1914 was going to be the last of its kind.

Well as the last joined schoolboy knows, the war for us started on August 4th, we being forced to declare war on Germany, it taking effect from midnight of that date.

I shall not easily forget the scene outside Buckingham Palace that night; the palace was surrounded by cheering, enthusiastic crowds, all shouting themselves hoarse and singing patriotic songs—in fact, doing all the things the phlegmatic Englishman is supposed never to do.

Next day I went to the city as usual, but was put to work on the new Government War Risks scheme, the insuring of ships at more reasonable rates than the insurance companies were able to give. That day and the next I spent answering questions for shippers and ship-owners of all nationalities and precious boring it was too!

Whether it was boredom or patriotism which drove me into the army I don't know, but next day, the 7th, I set off on a tour of the Territorial Regiment in London to try and get someone to take me in. The inns of court wouldn't look at anyone who hadn't previously been a soldier of some sort; I hadn't. So I went further up the street to the H.A.C., and found a crowd waiting outside the gate on a similar mission; but I was fortunately with a friend, Elwes, who was a nephew of the colonel of the regiment, Lord Denbigh, so after he had convinced the sentries of this fact—and nothing would make them believe it at first—we were admitted to the orderly room, and filled up various forms, and then were told to return next day, as the regiment was full up and awaiting war office sanction to form two new companies. In the light of future events it is hard to realise how difficult it was to get into the army in those days, even as a private soldier.

Next day, the 8th, we were duly elected members of the H.A.C., and paid our subscription of two guineas, for this was no ordinary regiment, but more like a soldiering club, where candidates had to be proposed and seconded by members.

I will not weary any possible readers of this book with much description of our training at home. We started drill next day. Personally, for many days I could do nothing right, and was always finding myself wandering aimlessly about the squad quite lost; arm drill defeated me entirely; but in course of time we got into it.

After a time, with things going badly in France and the German advance becoming daily more dangerous, the question arose as to whether Territorial Regiments should be sent to the front, they being formed for home service only. The law was that no Territorial Regiment could be sent abroad unless it volunteered, or, in other words, if a certain proportion of the men did so.

So we were asked to volunteer, and at first the response was disappointing, and it did not reach the required number. Next day Lord Denbigh addressed the battalion most eloquently, and put the case so well that 89 *per cent.*, if I remember correctly, volunteered.

As a result of this, we were ordered to hurry on our training with a view to proceeding to France at an early date. It was not thought that we could possibly be fit to go in under three or four months.

I was all this time in No. 2 Company, which was commanded by Captain Charles Whyte, than whom no one could have been kinder to the young and struggling soldier.

On the 12th September the battalion, under the command of Lieutenant-Colonel Treffry, was reviewed by the king preparatory to leaving for camp in Essex.

I had been on guard the night before, and had somehow omitted to find time to shave, so appeared on parade with a flowing beard, and was put gently but firmly into the rear rank!

After the inspection we marched through the city with fixed bayonets, thus exercising our ancient privilege, shared at that time with the 3rd Battalion Grenadier Guards, one battalion of Buffs, and by no one else. Whether we young soldiers, who found it difficult enough to carry a rifle without a bayonet on it, looked on the thing as a privilege or merely an additional burden, can be left to the imagination; however, we learnt later the value of old privileges and customs, together with that wonderful thing *esprit de corps*.

Our camp was in the park of Belhus Park, near Raynham, in Essex. We had a good many difficulties to contend with on arrival, the worst being a temporary shortage of food. We indulged in yet another of the private soldier's privileges, that of grousing, and loudly and longly we did it! But it did us no harm, and we soon settled down to the life happily enough.

We were not destined to make a long stay there, however, as on September 16th we got our orders to sail for France on the 18th. We were 1,000 strong, and we were ordered to send 800 men out, the remainder to follow as a first reinforcement as occasion demanded. We were all dead keen to go out, and it was whispered that the 800 best trained soldiers would go, so

9

I, knowing full well that I was one of the worst, if not actually the worst, spent a miserable day on the 17th, waiting for the announcement to be made as to who was going. Several times I waylaid the company commander and implored him not to leave me behind, but I didn't feel my chances were very good.

However, that evening I was called in and told that the company had been made up to strength without my valuable services, but that if I liked to take on the job of officer's servant and groom to the M.G. officer, I could go to France. Well, this was what the Yanks would call a bit of a "proposition." I didn't know one end of a horse from the other, and, except for fagging when a lower boy at Eton, had no experience in the servant line.

Anyhow, I decided to take the job, and reported, full of fear and trembling, to my new lord and master, Lieutenant Halliday, of the M.G. section. Later in the evening I was introduced to my horse, a long-legged chestnut with, mercifully, a reputation for quietude.

Next morning, the 18th, we left camp about 2 a.m. *en route* for Southampton, sailing about 4 p.m. At that time the Germans were getting on so fast that Havre was considered unsafe as a base, so we had to go all the way to St. Nazaire, at the mouth of the Loire, a sea journey of forty-eight hours.

Over that journey I would sooner draw a veil; suffice it to say that, whereas others remarked on the extraordinary calmness of the sea, I, after sleeping the first night in a pool of water on deck, spent the next twenty-four hours with my head well over the side, until rescued by the medical officer, a charming Irishman whose name I have forgotten, and taken below and restored to animation.

We arrived at St. Nazaire about 4.30 on the 20th, and had a wonderful reception from the inhabitants, the ship being pelted with fruit of all calibres.

We spent that night at a rest camp, so named, I suppose, from the fact that the crowd in the tents rendered any form of resting quite impossible! However, we had arrived in France, and we already began to think we were no end of heroes, and wrote home to our families to tell them so!

CHAPTER 2

At Various Bases

We stayed at St. Nazaire till the 23rd. St. Nazaire itself is rather a pleasant place, and the country round is pretty, but neither of these epithets apply in any degree to that rest camp in September, 1914.

The camp was full to breaking point—men from every conceivable regiment, all regular soldiers who had been washed back from the war on one pretext or another; we were so crowded that we had seventeen men sleeping in one ordinary bell tent; the days were boiling hot, and the nights bitterly cold.

I doubt if at any time during the war I was quite so miserable as at St. Nazaire. I had been taken away from my original platoon to do this servant job, and was thus separated from my friends, and doing work I didn't understand. The camp was filthy, and it seemed to be nobody's job to clean it; so altogether no one was sorry to move on.

At this point the battalion was split up, Numbers 1 and 2 Companies and the M.G. section, which I was with, went on to Le Mans to guard points of importance, the other two companies going to Nantes on similar work.

During all this time I was showing no skill whatever either as a groom or a servant; my horse showed a distressing lack of discipline, and my master's boots were never clean nor his shaving water hot. Consequently one day at Le Mans, the boots being even dirtier than usual and the shaving water even more gelid, my master, to whose patience up to now I pay a generous tribute, rose in his wrath and rebuked me; whereupon I applied, somewhat insubordinately I fear, to return to my old section in Number 2 Company. This was duly arranged, and everyone was very nice about it. I got back to my former friends, two of whom, Corkran and Elwes, I had known well before the war, and with this section I remained for the rest of my time with the regiment.

It cannot be said that our stay at Le Mans was particularly eventful. It is a large place, typically French, and pleasant enough.

On October 2nd the battalion was still further subdivided, and two platoons of No. 2 Company, which included ours, went on to Havre to do guards there. We were afterwards joined by the rest of the company.

Our job primarily was to guard the big shed at Havre through which the supplies for the front passed; this shed is known as the Hangar aux Cotons, and has ships on one side and the railway on the other.

We lived at this time in a camp by the docks, in between two sets of railway lines. It was not an ideal spot to spend the month of October in; others might have preferred shooting partridges in the Eastern Counties, but we got along well enough, and were becoming so hardened to discomfort that we really didn't mind it, and began to regard our previous pre-war luxurious living as belonging to some other world we had once lived in but should never visit again.

There wasn't much excitement at Havre. We had a few amusing incidents with drunken soldiery while doing our guards; they used to hate us, and call us——Territorials, and their language when marched off under escort would awaken the dead.

And so this ordinary routine of life went on, the monotony of guard mounting being relieved by an occasional fatigue, potato peeling, or some such congenial task. Occasionally men were sent off to guard trains going up to Railhead, and they were thought tremendous heroes if they contrived to see a shell burst during their travels.

There was much speculation during those early days as to whether we should ever be used as fighting troops, and there were actually people to be found who thought we should spend the whole war at the base, and although some timid souls contrived to do this, it was not to be our fate, as we discovered before very long.

We were ordered on the 26th, 100 men and three officers, to go to Abbeville, but on arriving there were sent on to Boulogne, where we were billeted in a large mill-shed which was already occupied by swarms of other men, chiefly A.S.C. At Boulogne we did various duties, including several funeral parties for men who had died of wounds in hospital.

It was here that we really got our first sight of the horrors of war, as the hospitals were all full, and car loads of fresh wounded were constantly arriving. I shall never forget the shiver which went down my back when doing a funeral party at the Casino hospital; on our way we passed a large marquee with its door open, and inside what looked like a whole lot of men sleeping wrapped up in blankets; and I remember thinking what a nasty, draughty place to put sick men to sleep in, when it dawned on me that they were all dead men waiting to be buried. One got hardened to this sort of thing, but it was unpleasant at the time.

On October 30th we moved on to St. Omer, and were quartered in the French barracks; here the battalion was re-formed, all the other companies returning. We did our first bit of trench digging outside St. Omer; we were supposed to be digging a line of defence, but I think it was only practice, and one which we discovered later was very useful. The entrenching tool was undoubtedly the most important implement of war in those days, and I'm not at all sure it didn't remain so to the end.

We heard the guns for the first time at St. Omer, and we were duly excited about it.

There were many rumours of our going up to fight, and when we heard that the London Scottish, who had been just a week ahead of us all along, had had a fight at Messines on November 1st, we knew our baptism of fire was not very far off.

CHAPTER 3

The War at Last

On November 5th "the day" arrived, and we went up to Bailleul, on the borders of France and Belgium, in motor-buses. Bailleul was then about six miles behind the firing line, where the desperate First Battle of Ypres was still going on; the Germans had been driven out only ten days before, and had stripped the place bare of provisions, though otherwise the place was not damaged. We felt we were properly "for it" now; the guns were roaring all the time, and aeroplanes buzzing about everywhere.

Next day we were marched up to the top of a hill to try and see something of the battle, but unfortunately there was a thick mist, and nothing could be seen; but it was very interesting, and one could but feebly imagine in those days what was happening away out in that mist, a great drama being played with no one to look on and applaud.

During our stay at Bailleul we saw one of our brigades, I think it must have been the 20th of the 7th Division, marching back to a well-earned rest after being relieved by the French. They had been in the trenches continuously for three weeks, and had all long beards; I remember being very much impressed by their terribly tired but still determined look, and wondering how we poor amateurs would look if we had to undergo the same ordeal.

On November 7th we moved to Estaires, some nine or ten miles south; we marched in the pitch dark, and the roads were terrible, all slimy mud, and altogether it was a very trying performance, being our first real active service march.

We spent two nights there, rather a jumpy time on the whole, as we expected to be pushed into the battle any moment; and the unknown is always alarming.

On the 9th we moved seven miles further South to a little place called Leslobes, due west of Neuve Chapelle, which was destined to mean so much to the British army later on. We were now attached to an Indian Brigade, and very fine fellows these old Indians were.

Next day General Willcocks, commanding the Indian contingent, inspected us, and said how glad they were to have us fighting with them.

The next few days we spent digging a reserve line west of Neuve Chapelle, about 1,000 yards from the front line. We used to get up in the dark and march four or five miles, and then dig all day and get back in the dark.

At this time something went wrong with the commissariat, and we got very little food, and no candles, so we never saw our billets in the light; consequently beards became the fashion, and there were some wonderful growths after our seven days there.

On November 10th we went up in support to some small night operation; there was a terrific cannonade, and I remember being almost inarticulate with fear, and quite unable to prevent my knees from knocking together.

I don't think it was till the 12th that we got our first shells close. It was not a nice sensation, and we dug that afternoon as we had never dug before.

The next day, the 13th, my birthday moreover, was our first real bad day, and we had our first casualties. I think they spotted us working; anyhow, there was a pretty continuous stream of bullets and shrapnel all the morning, and we spent the day in a ditch of most inadequate proportions; I remember also having a streaming cold that day too, so it was altogether a bit of a red letter day.

I have talked, I fear, rather lengthily about these opening days of our career, but, as the war was new to us then, as indeed to all but a very select few, these incidents have impressed themselves so on the mind that one cannot help recording them, though they are as nothing compared with other things later on which one hardly remembers.

On the 16th we returned to Bailleul, marching sixteen miles; we were not a very pretty looking lot by then, what with no shaving or washing, and not much chance to clean up; the soles of my boots were pretty well worn away, and I did the march practically on my socks, which, over pave roads, is no joke.

We rested till the 21st, when, prior to moving to Neuve Eglise, we were inspected by General Sir H. Smith-Dorrien, then commanding the 2nd Corps. He gave us a wonderful address, full of optimism, though I think he must have been intentionally over-optimistic so that we should not have the "wind up" during our first turn of duty in the trenches. He said he didn't think the war would last long, and that 85 *per cent,* of the German shells were "duds"; they must have improved their output soon after, as we found they burst only too well.

CHAPTER 4

In the Trenches: Wulverghem and Kemmel (to end of 1914)

Neuve Eglise was our next stop, a considerable village about three miles from the front line. It had an evil reputation, shells had been known to burst there, and at that time we didn't like shells much.

The idea was now to send us into the trenches by companies attached to regular battalions, so that we could learn the job without having much chance of doing the wrong thing. This system proved to be an excellent one, and as far as possible all new troops were introduced to the war in this way.

The company I was in left the village on the night of the 22nd for the reserve line of trenches; we got shelled on the way by 5.9, and very unpleasant it was, but a perfectly normal occurrence, as we learnt when we got older. One shell, I remember, set a house on fire, which impressed us very much at the time, especially as it was pitch dark.

Well, we got stuffed into funny little holes in the ground in the reserve line; they were the best we could do in the way of dugouts then; it was a terrible business getting into them, and well-nigh impossible to move once in. Fortunately the night was quiet, and only a few stray bullets reminded us that we were not sleeping peacefully in our beds in England.

Before dawn next day we moved up to the front line just east of Wulverghem in the Messines district. The war had pretty well subsided there, the Battle of Ypres was at length finished, and both sides, having failed to finish the war in three months as hoped for, settled down to that wonderful trench life which the world knows so well now.

It was a novelty then—not many people had been in the trenches; and now, having reached the foremost position, we may be excused that feeling of self-satisfaction which came over us.

There were several rows of stumpy willow trees in front of our trenches, and at night to the somewhat nervy sentry they looked like men advancing. Exactly how many massed attacks those willow trees carried out against our position that first night I don't know, but I don't think anyone missed seeing them on the move, in spite of a strict water diet.

Next morning at 9.45 a.m., and during the half-hour immediately following, we got our first real dressing down from the Hun. He turned a 5.9 battery on to our end of the trench, and for half-an-hour he sent continuous salvoes of four shells, some a few yards short of, some just over the trench.

For the information of those who have never been shelled—and I suppose there are some, even in these days—I would say that howitzer shells can be heard coming some seconds before their actual arrival, and this increases their horror enormously.

I thought my military career was going to be nipped in the bud that morning; it had frozen hard that night, and the shells blew great lumps of frozen earth at us, to say nothing of several enormous mangold wurzels, two of which landed in the same man's lap, much to his disgust.

We were very lucky, really, that day, as we had very few casualties, though the Royal Scots, to whom we were attached, were less fortunate. This little incident, small in itself, was enough to tell us that war was no child's game, and we left the trenches next day sadder and wiser men.

One thing which perhaps frightened us more than the shells even was that two old cows tried to get into our trench, already overcrowded; they came right up to the edge, and sniffed down on to us. I think they were afterwards killed by stray bullets.

We had another short spell at the Wulverghem position on the 27th, but that evening were unexpectedly relieved and sent further north, to a place called Westoutre; we had a long and weary march there; I have rarely felt so beat. When we halted, people went to sleep by the side of the road; some men even slept as they marched.

And so ended our apprenticeship, and thenceforward we worked as a complete unit, being part of the 7th Infantry Brigade of the 3rd Division, commanded then by Major-General Haldane. The 7th Brigade contained, if I remember right, a battalion of the Wiltshires, the Worcesters, the Royal Irish Rifles and the South Lancashires, all regular battalions, and already veterans.

On December 3rd we did a guard of honour to His Majesty on his first visit to the Front; he went up Sherpenberg Hill and watched our guns firing on to the Ypres Salient.

From now till the end of 1914 we did a regular roster of trench duty in front of Kemmel.

Our first experience there is perhaps worth talking about.

The weather had been terrible, continuous rain having fallen; the trenches were in an awful state. We had to relieve the Royal Scots Fusiliers of the 9th Brigade; they had had an awful time from the cold and wet; we found the front line trenches knee deep in water, and the support ones knee deep in mud. We had three men stuck up to their waists in mud for eight hours before they could be liberated; we tried to get them out with shovels, but the shovels got stuck too; and eventually two or three men rolled up their sleeves and loosened their feet by hand work.

We were supposed to have 48 hours there, and during that time people had been gradually dropping off, with numbed feet and general collapse. After 48 hours the relief was cancelled, and we were faced with another twenty-four hours; depressing, to say the least of it, and it had started raining again. I thought I was going all right, though not exactly enjoying life, until I was ordered to get out of my seat in the slime, and help carry in

19

the rations, and then my legs quite failed to function, and I sat gracefully down in the mud and stayed there.

Meanwhile, all the sick, and there were many, some half mad with cold and exposure, were collected in a little cottage just behind; thither I was escorted by some kind person, falling continually on the way, and found there a most wonderful company assembled—a collection of half dead, groaning humanity, some delirious, and all incapable of movement. I eventually got myself back with some other sufferers (we had found a bottle of rum, which I think must have had something to do with it) to a big farm house where the reserve companies were, and there we got every attention, and had a wonderful night's sleep on a hard floor.

Well, that wasn't a very pleasant start in the new sector, and we wondered if it would always be like that. I remember feeling then that I really couldn't last much longer, one felt so absolutely dead beat.

I daresay it doesn't sound as if we had done very much up to then, but we were all new to it all; there were no old soldiers to show us the way, and everyone knew so little about war then that we didn't get those many comforts which arrived in later years. We were pioneers of the Trench Life Movement, and we suffered for our temerity.

When out of the line we used to billet at Locre, a little village two miles west of Kemmel Hill, and not far from Bailleul, a place we used to go into as a kind of relaxation, to see a shop and a civilian again.

On the 14th December the 8th Brigade carried out an attack in front of Kemmel, and we were kept ready at Locre in reserve. The attack didn't accomplish much beyond showing the Boche we were still alive and ready for him. The Royal Scots and Gordons suffered especially heavily in the attack on Petit Bois. It was a difficult place to attack; the Boche commanded our trenches from the Wytschaete ridge, and although we got an even better view from Kemmel Hill, it didn't prevent him using his high ground.

It was rather a distressing little show altogether; attacking in those days was a terribly costly business; we knew so little about this unprecedented form of war.

And so things went on till the end of this very remarkable year.

We had Christmas Day in the front line, a thick fog making things even pleasanter.

We dropped our plum puddings in the mud, and altogether it was very dismal. However, the Boche was very quiet, and we had no shelling at all, so we were thankful for small mercies.

This Kemmel had been the scene of a bloodsome conflict between the French and the Boche, and the dead still lay thick on the ground; there was one particularly nasty group of Frenchmen caught by some wire and mown down.

Possibly the most dangerous time we had here was in billets in Kemmel; the Boche used to thrown 11-inch shells into the village, choosing our particular end almost invariably.

About this time Captain Whyte went home sick, and Captain Garnsey took over the company, and remained in command till I left.

CHAPTER 5

More Kemmel

Well, the New Year arrived, and was seen in in the customary fashion, and everyone hoped 1915 would see Germany beaten and peace restored; how wrong people were it is unnecessary to emphasise. Personally, I always thought the war had come to stay, and even when, many years later, they told me the Armistice had been signed, I didn't believe it.

The early days of 1915 found us still wallowing in the mud of Kemmel, and this we continued to do for some time.

It was very wearying work, cold and wet, and always expecting a shell to arrive, and going in and out of the trenches running the gauntlet of stray bullets; these "strays" were really the chief danger at this time. The Germans had a nasty habit of suddenly opening rapid rifle fire for no apparent reason; and the number of bullets which seemed just to miss me I shouldn't like to recount. I remember one particularly famous bullet which several people claimed as having just missed them; I thought it had missed the end of my nose by a hairsbreadth; the man behind had a similar idea, and so on; this shows how difficult it was to say exactly where they came.

Verey lights, or star shells as we used to call them, were a nuisance too, especially if they fell over one's head, and they showed up reliefs coming up quite clearly, and it meant flopping in the mud as soon as one was seen coming.

On January 12th our first reinforcement of 400 men arrived from England, among them those unlucky ones who just got left behind in September. Their arrival rather cheered us up, as it amused us showing them round the war and playing the veteran to them.

In February the Boche began to wake up a bit, chiefly further north round Ypres, and we got quite a lot of shelling, though no actual attack in our part. But we felt the effects of his Ypres attacks in that troops from our division had to be sent north to help, and consequently we had to do longer spells in the trenches, and reliefs became very problematical, and many intended reliefs had to be cancelled at the last moment. Nothing was more disappointing to the tired soldier, looking forward to a wash and a bit of sleep and a walk to stretch one's legs, than to be expecting relief and then not to get it; this we had to put up with often in the early days of 1915.

In February we moved slightly north to other trenches known as the K trenches. There was one particularly nasty line there known as the K support pits, being a line of dugouts, flush with the ground, into which one crawled and lay there throughout the hours of light, getting up at night for a little exercise among the bullets. That place was an awful nightmare, and I was thankful my platoon only went there once.

We didn't stay very long at a time in the front lines, coming back to a large building known as the "Creamery," only about half a mile back; it was quite intact, and held about half a battalion; half the battalion used to be there and half in front. It always seemed a marvel to me why they never shelled the old Creamery, as they used to plaster the farms all round. The usual explanations for buildings being let off was that they had belonged to Germans in peace time; I expect it was flattened out before the war finished. I never went to that part after leaving the H.A.C.

The last week of February we returned to our old trenches, the F's,. and it seemed like going home, almost.

About this time we were lent to the 85th Brigade, who had come south after a bad time at Ypres, and were much reduced in strength.

At the beginning of March we had about our longest tour of duty in the line. My platoon lived in a redoubt, 300 yards from the front, for nine days on end; we felt like caged animals before the end. Before we were relieved an attack was carried out by the 7th Brigade as a side show to the Neuve Chapelle battle further south.

We held the actual line, and the other brigade was to pass through us to the attack. Our new 15-inch howitzer was fired for the first time in this show.

The attack was carried out by the Worcester and Wiltshire Regiments; they formed up on the night of 11-12th March, with the idea of attacking at dawn on the 12th with the aid of a heavy bombardment. However, there was such a thick fog in the morning, the same fog which muddled things so for us at Neuve Chapelle, that the attack had to be put off, and didn't actually take place till 4.10 in the afternoon. It was preceded by what we thought then to be a terrific bombardment, and we kept our heads pretty low in our redoubt to dodge the German reply, which, however, was luckily very feeble.

The attack was not a success, though carried out most gallantly. Certain trenches were taken, and the Boche got pretty well disorganised, and started off to Wytschaete village behind; there appeared to be some misunderstanding between our gunners and our infantry, a thing which unfortunately did occur from time to time, and the captured trenches were so heartily shelled by both sides that our men had reluctantly to withdraw; it is doubtful anyhow if the trenches could have been held, as the front of the attack was so limited that they must have been taken in flank if the Germans had any go in them at all, and in those days they were full of it.

Our losses were considerable, and it may appear to the uninitiated that the whole thing was a waste of life, but I imagine it must really have succeeded in its primary object, that of preventing reinforcements from our sector being sent to Neuve Chapelle, where the real blow was being delivered.

On the 13th we were still in our redoubt, with no prospect of being anything else; all the rest of the battalion had been doing inter-company reliefs, but there weren't quite enough men to relieve us too; however, on the 13th evening, as motley a collection of soldiers as ever took the battlefield came up to relieve us; they were transport men, cooks, drummers and what not, men whose daily life lay behind the lines, but they all counted, and they gave us that rest for which we had been longing so many days.

We went to Kemmel that night, and were to have gone further back next day, but the Germans tactlessly started their counter blow to our offensive, and selected St. Eloi, just next door to us, as the venue. Result, instead of going back we went forward again. However, on the 16th we were relieved by the 7th Brigade, who were by then rested from their efforts of the 12th, and we went back to camp at Westoutre.

It may be of interest to some to say that it was at this stage that hand bombing first came in; the Germans had been doing it for a little time already, but our first bombing instruction took place in March, 1915.

We had a week's rest at Westoutre. The time passed pleasantly enough; we played stump cricket matches, although somewhat early in the year for the game, and really rather enjoyed life.

We had meanwhile returned to our old love, the 7th Brigade, and it was with them we did our next period in the trenches.

Chapter 6

St. Eloi and the Cadet School

On March 23rd we went up to the trenches at St. Eloi, taking over the line as it was after the very gallant attack by, I think, an Irish battalion, but I fear I forget which, had practically restored the situation after the German attack on the 15th.

The commanding officer (Lieutenant-Colonel Treffry, who had been with us since the start) addressed the battalion before we went up, and warned us of the importance of the position, and exhorted us to be specially on the alert owing to recent German attacks and the prospect of more to come.

The position of St. Eloi was this—the actual village, which was only a few houses., was in No Man's Land; the famous mound, a tumulus of earth, was held by the Germans, and overlooked our lines, although a constant target for our artillery; the village and the mound had been in our hands before the 15th. One curious feature of No Man's Land was a derelict London motor bus which had been used to rush up reinforcements and had fallen a victim to a German shell.

We got in for a good deal of shelling, a new and very small type making its first appearance.

We held the village of Voormezeele, 1,000 yards behind, and our reserves were billeted there in cellars. The village was a complete wreck, and I remember going over the churchyard there and being disgusted by seeing the tombs all blown up and bones lying about everywhere.

After our tour of duty here we went back to Dickebusch,

some two and a half miles back; this village was then more or less intact, but was destined later to be flattened out.

Life was pretty strenuous now, as while out of the line we had to go up every night and dig a reserve line of trenches to bar the next German attack if it came.

I think it may be said that at this time we were in rather a precarious state; we still had only the old army, plus a few Territorials, and the Germans appeared to be strong everywhere, and it was reasonable to suppose that they might start a big offensive any moment. And so it was that the few troops we had got—and the battle of Neuve Chapelle had lost us a lot—had to work terrifically hard, with no prospect of anything else until such time as Kitchener's army, as everyone called it, was ready to come to our assistance.

As it turned out, things quietened down for a bit, and we had no trouble at St. Eloi. The Germans were evidently planning that devilishly cunning attack carried out at Ypres at the end of April, when they first introduced poisoned gas into warfare, thus rendering it even more horrible than before.

On April 3rd I paid my first visit to Ypres; it was more or less a "joy-ride," and I had to get leave to go there. The town, though badly damaged in parts, was still a thriving community, and was full of people, the square being full of street vendors. We had an excellent lunch at a restaurant, and saw all over the place. It was a very different Ypres to the one we got to know so well in 1916 and 1917. The cathedral was pretty well ruined even then, and the beautiful Cloth Hall was being used as a stable for mules.

Next day I said farewell to the battalion, on going to a cadet school prior to getting a commission.

I should like, before going on to other matters, to pay a humble tribute to this very wonderful battalion; it had an *esprit de corps* second only to that of the brigade of Guards, and it was that, coupled with the way everyone tried to help everyone else, that brought us through those early and most trying days. Personally, I never wish to be treated more kindly and more patiently by my superiors than I was in those days. The battalion had many difficulties, but never received anything but praise from the higher authorities.

I left the battalion with my old friends Corkran and Elwes, the former destined for the Grenadiers, as I was myself, and the latter for the Coldstream. No one could have had two stauncher friends than these two during these times, and of them more anon.

We went to our cadet school first at Bailleul, and afterwards moving to Blendecques, near St. Omer, and a very delightful change it was too, and we all enjoyed it very much. I unluckily caught German measles three-quarters way through the course, and had to return to complete it, thus being longer getting my commission than I should have.

Included in the course were two short visits to the trenches to study life there from the officer's point of view. Owing to my measles I got in for three visits, and went successively to Wulverghem, attached to a battalion of the Staffs. Regiment, Ploegsteert Wood, then most peaceful, attached to the 8th Battalion Worcester Regiment, and Armentières, if anything more peaceful still, attached to the 2nd Battalion Welsh Fusiliers.

On the 26th May I left for England, a full-blooded ensign in the Grenadiers, and there was no prouder man in the British army.

CHAPTER 7

Early Days as a Grenadier

After a short three days' leave, which was all one got in those days, I returned to France to try and be an officer.

It was with no little trepidation that I started on my new career. Guardsmen aren't made in a day, and I was one of a very small number who joined the regiment in France direct from another regiment without first passing through the very necessary moulding process at Chelsea Barracks.

Thus, it may be imagined that I committed many sins when I first started, and but for the extraordinary energy always shown by the commanding officer (Major Jeffreys, as he was then) in all matters concerning the regiment, I might never have learnt my lesson at all. As it was, he set to work to try and turn me into a soldier, and I am afraid it must have been tedious work. It meant my having special instruction three times a day when we were out of the line, and I confess I hated it at the time, but have never regretted it since, and have never ceased to be thankful for the interest taken in me at that time.

I joined the 2nd Battalion Grenadier Guards on the 31st May. They had just finished seven days' rest after the battle of Festubert, and on arriving at Vendin, near Bethune, where I was told I should find them, I found they had gone south that morning to Noeux-les-Mines. However, luckily I found part of the transport still there, and I made friends with the post sergeant, who gave me a tin of Maconochie for my lunch, and conducted me to a seat on a G.S. wagon; thus we arrived at Noeux that afternoon.

I was posted to No. 3 Company, commanded by Captain Ivor Rose, the other officers being Armar Corry and my old friend Corkran, who was most useful in telling me what to do and what not to.

We were to remain at Noeux till June 6th, when we were to take over a line of trenches from some Territorials, who had recently relieved the French there.

On the 4th June we had an Old Etonian dinner of some sixty odd people from the 4th (Guards) Brigade. This brigade formed part of the 2nd Division, under Major-General Home, and consisted of our battalion, the 2nd and 3rd Battalions Coldstream, and the 1st Battalion Irish Guards, plus the 1st Battalion Hertfordshire Regiment attached.

On the 5th Captain Rose went sick with fever, and Captain Ralph Cavendish took over the Company, and I remained under him the rest of my time with the Battalion. The other company commanders at this time were Major Lord Henry Seymour, Major de Crespigny, Captain P. A. Clive. Major Jeffreys had just got command, succeeding Colonel Wilfred Abel Smith, who was killed at Festubert.

I doubt very much if a finer battalion than the 2nd Battalion at this time has ever existed; to me, of course, it was a perfect revelation.

We took over our new line on the 6th, in front of Cambrin, and the brigade held it till the 27th. Although this was stationary warfare as far as we were concerned, there were many interesting, not to say dangerous, moments during this tour of duty.

Our first job there was to cut the grass in front of our trenches; this had grown so high that it was impossible to see what was going on in No Man's Land. It was whilst in charge of a grass cutting party that poor Reggie Corkran received the wound from which he died a few days later. The Germans sent over a Verey light and spotted the party working, and opened rifle fire on them, wounding Corkran in the thigh; we never thought for a moment that the wound was dangerous, and his death came as a great shock. I need hardly say I felt his loss very keenly; we had been together during the whole campaign up till then, and no more unselfish or charming person ever lived; during the whole of that very trying first winter there was never a word of complaint and never a suspicion of grousing from him, and goodness knows, the rest of us groused enough; and he was always a shining example of what a good soldier ought to be. Had he lived he would have done great things for the regiment.

When not actually in the front lines we used to billet in Sailly Labourse, a straggling mining village of no particular importance, and we were comfortable enough there in spite of occasional shellings.

The trenches we occupied were remarkably good, with most luxurious, if somewhat unsafe, dugouts. I fancy the French had had a pretty quiet winter there, and had made themselves thoroughly comfortable.

In the second week of June there were rumours of another attack coming off, and the brigadier, Lord Cavan, lectured all the officers of the brigade on the offensive spirit; it is interesting to note that he quoted from an article from the "Round Table," describing that article as quite the best and most sensible thing he had yet seen written about the war. The writer of that article joined the brigade as a junior ensign in the 2nd Battalion the next week, in the person of 2nd Lieut. E. W. M. Grigg.

It appeared that the French were contemplating operations in the Souchez district, and required assistance from us; so the 4th Corps, on our left about Givenchy, were to carry out an attack, and if it was successful it was to spread to our part of the line.

Well, this attack took place on June 15th, and failed; it was continued on the 16th, but came to nothing; it was only a local attack, and any ground gained was lost again by bombing attacks. Our artillery support was poor too, through no fault of our gunners, but from the very lamentable shortage of shells at that time, a shortage which cramped us at every turn.

The Germans fired 5.9 high explosive, and bigger, at us, and we could only reply with mountain guns and 18-pounder shrapnel. The reason of this shortage is nothing to do with me, but it was the cause of our complete inactivity during the summer of 1915.

On the 19th June I was sent on my first patrol with a sergeant and three men; our job was to spy out the land round the new earth-work which the Germans had just prepared, and which we called the Hohenzollern Redoubt. This place was destined to become famous later, but was then in its infancy. I don't claim to have found out a great deal about it that night, but we got to know all about the beastly place later in the year, as a later chapter will reveal.

On the 27th we were relieved, if I remember right, by the 1st Division, and we went back for a week or ten days' rest, first at Fouquereil and then at Oblinghem, and finally Annezin, all three places being just outside Bethune.

On the 29th June the brigadier left to command a division, and General Feilding took his place. The latter had commanded the 3rd Battalion Coldstream.

CHAPTER 8

Cuinchy and Givenchy

Our rest round Bethune passed off uneventfully, and on July 5th we returned once more to the war.

We were to hold a line just north of our previous position, and just in front of what was once the village of Cuinchy. The brigade had had previous experience of the place earlier in the year, and its reputation was none too pleasant.

It was one of those places where the German was very close, and where there was much mining going on, and where one expected to go up in the air at any moment. Enormous trench mortar bombs used to arrive at intervals, and one never quite knew what to expect. I didn't get in for very much of this Cuinchy place, as I developed a disease which was finally diagnosed as nettle rash, and retired to St. Omer labelled "Measles." There I stayed till the 17th, bored beyond measure, and I was only too glad to get back to the war again.

We used to do two days in the front lines and two in Bethune. Bethune was a comfortable place to billet in, and was very little knocked about; shells arrived spasmodically, but chiefly round the station, which one could avoid; they occasionally had a go at the square; and the only thing to do then was to stop indoors and pray one might not arrive on the roof.

Apart from this, Bethune was a cheerful place, and a great shopping centre for troops from miles around; it also had quite a respectable cocktail establishment known as the "Globe," where the drunken soldiery used to foregather.

On the 21st July, the Worcester Regiment, of another brigade, relieved us, and we returned for eight days to Bethune, till it took us for the Givenchy line.

Now, Givenchy was no joke; it was like Cuinchy, only the things which one dreaded happening at the latter actually did happen at Givenchy. The battalion was in the neighbourhood for sixteen days, and had some 200 casualties during that time, simply holding the trenches.

There was a continuous hail of trench mortar bombs all night, and usually a mine or two went up in the early morning. These mines were luckily generally a bit short of their mark, and it was the trench mortars which did the real damage. It was a perfect nightmare there, and was one of the most trying places I was at the whole war, possibly only beaten by the Hohenzollern Redoubt later in the same year.

All mines which went up had to be reported by telephone, and I remember standing with my company commander one grey dawn when one happened just in front of us, and I was left to see if another did, and sure enough it did, and worse than the last; it is a most curious sensation, and one denied to those who came later to the war, as mining died out towards the end.

We had several officer casualties. Captain Percy Clive was partially buried by a mine and also wounded, and went down; the same mine buried Crookshank, one of his subalterns, for twenty minutes; the latter didn't seem to worry at all at his misfortune, and carried on at duty as soon as he had been disinterred, minus, however, his cap, and the one he borrowed from a private soldier didn't fit, and this was his only trouble!

Arthur Wiggins, who had joined my company shortly before then, took command of No. 2 Company in succession to Clive.

On August 10th there was an unlucky incident. We had been bombing the enemy all day from a sap-head, trying to prevent him building a new forward trench, the party consisting of the bombing officer, G. Bailey, and one officer from the front line company, and one other rank. The operation was successful enough, but just before being relieved by the Irish Guards Bailey was killed by a bomb, and Armar Corry, the other officer there, badly wounded in the face. It was a most unlucky thing, and unlucky for the battalion, as Gerry Bailey was one of the most popular men in the battalion, and quite without fear.

On the same day Captain Derriman, who had left the battalion a few weeks before to become staff captain, died of wounds received walking along the La Bassée road. Shortly after, E. G. Williams, while doing a trench mortar course, was killed accidentally by a premature explosion.

So rather a gloom came over the battalion, and it was with few regrets that we turned our backs on Givenchy; the only redeeming feature of this sector was the village of Le Preol on the La Bassée canal, where we used to go when not actually in the front lines. It was very peaceful, and might have been miles from the war, though actually only two miles. Warfare here was essentially close, and at Le Preol we felt perfectly safe.

The drums of the battalion arrived when we were there, and there was great excitement at hearing them play again.

Wilfred Beaumont-Nesbitt joined the company at Le Preol.

We returned to Bethune on the 15th, and on the 19th we started on our march back to the St. Omer district to form the Guards' Division. We thus left the 2nd Division, and the 4th Brigade was no more; there were many regrets at the change, and we lost our old friends the Herts. Regiment, who had shared our troubles so long.

We did the journey in three stages, staying nights at Ham-en-Artois and Renescure en route, arriving on the 21st at Houlle, having marched past Sir John French at St. Omer.

On the 24th we moved to Campagne les Boulonais, and incidentally had one of the hottest marches I remember. Here we stayed while the division was formed.

Various changes had taken place in the battalion. Lord H. Seymour had become second in command; Major de Crespigny had gone to the 1st Battalion as second in command, the companies being commanded by (1) Captain J. N. Buchanan, (2) Captain Wiggins, (3) Captain Cavendish, (4) Captain Kingsmill.

CHAPTER 9

The Guards' Division and the Battle of Loos

The idea of forming a Guards' Division emanated, I believe, from the late Lord Kitchener.

The change was not popular at first, as people thought that if the division took a bad knock, the Brigade of Guards might be finished, but as it turned out the division took many bad knocks, but always came up smiling; and I don't think anyone will question the success of the new idea or wish that it had been otherwise.

In order to bring the division up to strength, *i.e.*, twelve ordinary battalions and one pioneer, the 3rd Battalion Grenadiers, the only remaining regular battalion, was sent out from London, and the regiment formed a 4th Battalion, which arrived shortly after. The Coldstream formed a 4th Battalion, which became a Pioneer Battalion; the Irish Guards formed a 2nd Battalion; and, lastly, the new Welsh Guards' Battalion was sent out.

Thus the three Brigades were made up as under:—

The 1st Guards' Brigade (the old 4th Brigade):
2nd Batt. Grenadier Guards,
2nd Batt. Coldstream,
3rd Batt. Coldstream,
1st Batt. Irish Guards,
under Brig.-Gen. Feilding.

The 2nd Guards' Brigade (remains of the old 1st Infantry Brigade):
3rd Batt. Grenadier Guards,
1st Batt. Coldstream,
1st Batt. Scots Guards
2nd Batt. Irish Guards,
under Brig.-Gen. Ponsonby.

The 3rd Guards' Brigade (remains of the old 20th Brigade):
1st Batt. Grenadier Guards,
4th Batt. Grenadier Guards,
2nd Batt. Scots Guards,
1st Batt. Welsh Guards,
under Brig.-Gen. Heyworth; with Lord Cavan commanding the division.

Having concentrated, we set to work to train for the new great offensive which everyone was talking about, but of which, officially, no one knew anything.

Meanwhile, a good many of us got some leave, and I went home for a week in September.

We stayed at Campagne till the 22nd September, and we had a very good rest; it was pretty country and away from the sound of guns, and we were thoroughly recuperated by the time the Loos battle came on. It was as well we had this rest, as there were hard times in store for us.

We received reinforcements in officers and men, and my company officers then consisted of Cavendish, B. Ponsonby, Nesbit, Ingleby and myself.

By the 22nd September we were ready for anything, and really keen to get at the German again.

The great battle of Loos was due to start on the 25th; much was expected from this battle; experts thought it might materially shorten the war. Maps of country far behind the German lines were issued, country not actually seen by us till after the Armistice. Douai was to be our first real stopping place, Berlin our final objective!

That the battle was a bitter disappointment need hardly be said, but we learnt many lessons from it, and it was not in vain.

We left Campagne on the evening of the 22nd, all our movements being by night, and slept at Coyecques, leaving next day for Westrehem, where we stayed two nights. All night long on the 24-25th night we could hear the roar of artillery, a roar such as we had never heard before.

Next day was the great day, and we rose early for Ferfay, a place some ten miles from the line.

We were G.H.Q. reserve, and meant to be pushed through the gap when made.

Meanwhile, the weather broke, as it generally did when we contemplated a "push," and we had a wet and miserable march on from Ferfay to Noeux-les-Mines, where we spent the night of the 25-26th. The roads were blocked with troops and transport, and altogether we were pretty weary by the time we arrived; this was unfortunate, as we had been so full of buck before.

Next morning we were at half-an-hour's notice to move, and spent a most jumpy morning, expecting to move off any moment.

Waiting to "pop the parapet" is one of the richer sensations of warfare, and perhaps the most trying of the lot.

However, at 1 p.m. on the 26th we got on the move, going up by platoons, through our old friend Sailly Labourse, which had an unwontedly busy look about it, and on through Vermelles.

We passed little knots of men on the way up, and one felt that one was in for some dirty work—shells bursting everywhere ahead confirmed this impression.

Vermelles village was a wonderful sight; it made me think, though I had never seen it, of Hampstead Heath on Bank Holiday; crowds everywhere, horses, carts, everyone seemed to have gathered there for the show; Generals with their staffs looking through their field glasses, wounded men walking back, some unwounded men, I fear, running back; fresh troops coming up, and an occasional shell bursting in the middle of the lot. Here the Hampstead Heath idea fades into the background; there were dead horses everywhere in the road, and the scene was really most exhilarating.

Vermelles, when we knew it in June, had been a place one crept through under cover of darkness, and here were all these thousands swarming in daylight; it seemed all wrong.

When we got through the village we were told things were going better; a regular battalion of Black Watch and some others had done a good attack and restored the situation, so we were to take up a position just in rear of the front line for the night.

Next day things were fairly quiet in our part of the line, but we could see attacks going on on our left at Fosse 8, a large slag heap which changed hands several times, and we could see lines of men attack and get driven back and then return again to the attack; they must have suffered terribly. That afternoon, about 4 p.m., the 2nd and 3rd Guards' Brigades carried out an attack on our right against Hill 70 and the chalk pits and Puits 14 Bis; this attack became famous owing to the wonderful steadiness of the troops under terrible fire, and those who watched it were amazed. Our brigade did not move, but held a defensive position on the flank of the attack.

The 2nd and 3rd Brigades had terrible losses, but achieved a certain measure of success, and at any rate put things straight in that part of the line.

I did not actually see anything of the attack, so have not described it fully, as I wish only to write of things I actually saw myself in the war, so it must not be thought that this was only a small affair, but it was indeed one of the most glorious of the division's achievements, and will be remembered as the first of its many successes.

The next three nights we dug like mad consolidating the new line, and the whole division was relieved on the night 30th-1st October by another division, exactly which I can't remember, except that we were relieved by a battalion of Royal Fusiliers, and the company taking over from us was commanded by a man who had been at Eton with me, Elliot Cooper by name; he afterwards got a V.C. and was killed.

We marched back to Mazingarbe more dead than alive. We had had no sleep up there, and although not actually attacking, we had a pretty hard time, and not without anxiety.

We only got two days' rest at Mazingarbe, and then went forward again.

At this time my next change of Battalion took place; we were ordered to send two officers to the 3rd Battalion and two to the 4th to help replace their casualties; and I was ordered to go to the 3rd with Hermon-Hodge, Sitwell and Ingleby going to the 4th. I was very disappointed at leaving the battalion, but I was still junior ensign, so I suppose it took me to go, but it was a bitter moment.

CHAPTER 10

The 3rd Battalion and the Hohenzollern Redoubt

I arrived at the 3rd Battalion on October 3rd. They had just moved up again, and were in trenches and cellars round Vermelles. Colonel Noel Corry was commanding, with Major Montgomery second in command. The companies were commanded by (1) Wolridge Gordon, (2) Walker, (3) Powell, (4) Dowling. I was posted to No. 2 Company, the only other subaltern there being Alec Agar-Robartes.

I must say I found the 3rd Battalion rather young soldiers in the art of trench warfare; this was only natural, as it was their first attempt at it. Some of the officers and men had been out before, but in the days of open warfare.

I found the company officers just about to start lunch, with no appliances for doing so, and only old Maconochie stew to eat; in the 2nd Battalion, through long months of practice, we had our messing arrangements well-nigh perfect, and lived pretty sumptuously, or there was trouble for the Mess President if we didn't!

Company H.Q. were then in an open trench, but I suggested that a cellar nearby in Vermelles would be more comfortable, and eventually we moved there, not that it was exactly a bed of roses there, as there were two 6-inch howitzers about ten yards from our window, and the shock when they fired nearly blew one out of the cellar.

Well, we had two nights of this place, and then moved up to the front system; Nos. 3 and 4 Companies were to hold the front line, No. 1 in close support, and ourselves in reserve.

The relief was not too well organised, again owing to lack of experience in such matters, and we took most of the night finding our new position. This position was in the western face of the Hohenzollern Redoubt; the remainder of the redoubt was in the hands of the Germans. We had the 3rd Battalion Coldstream, of the 1st Brigade, on our right; the Germans were on our immediate left, and further to the left came the 3rd Brigade.

It was not a pleasant position to hold, especially for troops who were making their bow to trench warfare.

I say all this leading up to the events of the 8th of October, a day never to be forgotten by those who were present at the Hohenzollern Redoubt; the battalion lost its name pretty thoroughly, but I honestly believe that if any other battalion had been there precisely the same would have occurred.

On October 7th No. 2 Company was ordered to relieve No. 4, who had had a good deal of shelling, and had asked to be relieved; No. 3 remained on the right front, and No. 1 stayed in its old position. This front trench was known as Big Willie, and was about the worst trench I have ever been in. It was much too broad, and had suffered a lot from shell fire. Our right flank, as I have said, was secure, but our left was in the air, with but a single block between us and the enemy. We had a strong bombing post there, consisting of all our expert bombers under Lieutenant A. Anson, the bombing officer; their job was to watch that flank, while the rest of the battalion watched their front.

The next morning the German artillery was pretty active, and they kept up a spasmodic shelling on the battalion front; however, we never suspected anything unusual, and I remember lunching that day with Walker, Alec Robartes, Arthur Anson and Williams, the M.G. officer. Suddenly, before we had finished, there came a cry of "All bombers to the left!" Anson rushed off to the left flank, and that was the last we ever saw of him.

Meanwhile, the sentries in front reported a frontal attack,

and we lined the parapet and blazed off our rifles and machine guns, and had a real good shoot and beat them off all right, but far from our troubles being over, we suddenly saw the Germans coming down the trench on our left flank; they had apparently killed all our bombers, and were bombing us with their little stick bombs down the trench.

It was a very awkward position; all available bombs were sent up to the left, but most of them were undetonated; we were thus completely caught in a trap, and the company was gradually forced back on to No. 3 Company. Lieutenant Williams mounted a machine gun in a communication trench and carried on most gallantly until shot through the head and killed. Sergeant Kendrick carried on, but received the same fate; meanwhile, we had lined a platoon up along this communication trench and poured volley after volley at the Germans who were attacking strongly. All this time the earth shook with exploding bombs, and it was very difficult to think of what to do.

We three officers got together and decided we would try and turn about and charge up the trench, but this would have meant an attack on a one-man frontage against an enemy well armed with bombs, and must have failed; anyhow, there was such a noise that no verbal orders could be heard, and the pushing back process continued. At one point the three officers got left behind trying to find a solution, and had to double over the open to avoid capture; in doing this the other two were hit, Walker in the back and Robartes in the face.

The resulting confusion and congestion in the trench had forced No. 3 Company out at their end and back along another communication trench towards the second line, and after about half an hour of this, the Germans had got possession of the whole of the battalion's front line, leaving the 3rd Battalion Coldstream with their left in the air. As it happened, as we had run out of bombs, our vacating the trench was the best and perhaps the only solution of the problem, as it left an unit which had not been engaged, and which had its full complement of bombs intact, a clear field for a counter bombing attack, and of this opportunity they were not slow to take advantage, Sergeant Brooks organising a party and regaining the whole of the lost trench and inflicting terrible casualties on the Germans.

While this was going on, we were reorganising, and had got together a party for the counter attack under Lieutenant Eaton and Lieutenant Gunnis; on their arriving in the front they found that the Coldstream had pretty well finished the job, but our party was able to help them complete it by a further supply of bombs.

The Germans then fled in all directions, and our No. 1 Company in support had a fine overhead shoot, and wrought great destruction on the Germans. Thus, before dark the situation was entirely restored, and the battalion re-occupied its old trench, or what remained of it. This trench was practically blown flat, and was like a shambles, a horrible sight with masses of dead and debris everywhere; that night was spent digging it out.

We discovered after that this attack was part of the enemy's big counter effort to the battle of Loos, and aimed at regaining all he had lost and perhaps more; that it failed was no small achievement for our side.

The company spent next day in a reserve trench, recovering from the shock of the day before. I think we all felt a bit dazed, and were glad enough when we were relieved by the 4th Battalion in the evening and returned to Vermelles.

The battalion had lost heavily; my company had over fifty casualties.

Next day, the 10th, a big draft arrived from England, and we were brought up to strength again. Captain E. O. Stewart took over command of No. 2, vice Captain Walker, who went to hospital wounded, and Lt. P. M. Walker also joined from home.

We stayed at Vermelles till the 12th. There were many fatigue parties to the front line, chiefly carrying up gas cylinders, but Walker insisted on taking charge of them all and letting me have a bit of rest, for which I was most grateful. In fact, the new people just joined did everything they could to lighten our task and give us a chance to get ourselves right again.

On the 12th the division was relieved, and went back to various little villages seven or eight miles in rear.

We went to a place called Drouvin, where we set to work to re-organise. We had very little time, as the 46th Division, who relieved us, were to do a gas attack on the 13th with the idea of clearing the whole of the Hohenzollern Redoubt and getting possession, if possible, of Fosse 8, known as "The Dump"; and we were held in readiness to help them either in pushing the attack or consolidating the ground gained.

Their attack unluckily failed, though they made two gallant attempts; and no ground was gained, and the losses were great.

On the 15th the battalion returned to the front lines, just to the right of the scene of our previous troubles.

Lord Frederick Blackwood joined the company on the way up, so we had now four officers.

This relief, too, went badly, and there was much shelling on the way, and I gather the Germans tried a small attack; anyhow, it wasn't till we had suffered hours of misery that we arrived in the correct trench; we were at first in support in a most unhealthy trench, and we were heavily shelled by large stuff next morning, and we looked to be in for more trouble.

On the 16th the company was ordered up to the front support line preparatory to doing a bombing attack. The 1st Battalion Coldstream were holding the actual front line, a piece of the old west face of the redoubt; a communication trench partially dug connected us with them. On their right were the Germans, and then came the 2nd Battalion Scots Guards, and our job was to dig through the communication trench, advance up it to the Coldstream trench, and bomb to the flank and connect up with the Scots Guards, who would also bomb inwards. Why it was decided to do it this way I don't know; perhaps it was to give the battalion a chance of distinguishing itself after its bad luck of the week before; it would have seemed simpler for the Coldstream, who were already in position, to do the attack. Our job of finishing the communication trench was extremely difficult; work could only be done at night, and then one could only sap and not dig from the top, and the Germans were only a few yards off, and it meant certain death to show oneself. Moreover, the attack was due next morning, at dawn; added to this, we had to organise the attack in complete darkness, with fatigue parties and wiring parties continually passing up and down the trench and blocking it. I was to lead it with the actual bombers, the remainder of the company was to follow in rear, the other three companies being ready to follow if required.

The trouble of the sap still remained, and it seemed impossible to get it done in the time, and we sent messages back more than once to this effect; however, we were told it had to be done, but it proved too much, and when I say that the sap wasn't finished till the night of the 18th, I think it will be understood that we were given a quite impossible task.

Result, of course, more loss of name to the battalion; the Coldstream did the attack, and altogether things weren't too bright for us.

The attack took place at dawn as arranged, and was pretty well successful; we were to co-operate, if needed, by overhead fire; it was a wonderful sight, the continuous bursting of bombs, and it was difficult to tell what was going on.

Meanwhile, the German artillery got to work, and for the rest of that morning and up to about three in the afternoon they gave our trenches the most awful pounding I have ever experienced. No. 1 Company had fifty casualties from shells that morning, men being continually buried. We were a bit more lucky in front, as the shooting wasn't so accurate, but it was a terrible day, and it seemed it would never end; the behaviour of the men under the ordeal was beyond praise.

Lord F. Blackwood had been wounded and shell-shocked the night before, and was sent off to hospital; Lieutenant Walker, whose first fight it was, after working like a slave all the night before and that day, collapsed in a heap at the bottom of the trench, and also went to hospital; that left only Captain Stewart and myself.

That night the 1st Battalion Scots Guards relieved us, and we went to some reserve trenches in front of Vermelles, where it was quiet but uncomfortable. Three nights later we were in the front line again; this time we had more sapping to do. We were trying to dig a new front line about thirty yards from the Germans; it was most dangerous work, as the German was very much on the alert. It was altogether an unpleasant trench; it was known as the Kaiserin trench, and was lined with dead, our own and the 46th Division, who had attacked on the 13th. I remember one dead man being set on fire by a Verey light, and a perfect fusillade being started by the ammunition in his pouches going off.

It took each company in turn to go and dig at the trench; it took us on the night of the 22nd, and we got the job done and really got some credit this time.

Next day the 4th Battalion relieved us, and so good-bye to the Hohenzollern Redoubt, and we never went there again.

I think that month was the worst we ever had; we were kept continually at it, and at such close quarters.

Major Montgomery was killed superintending the digging; his was a great loss; there was no more popular officer in the regiment.

On the 23rd we went back to Sailly Labourse, and I remember drinking a bottle of champagne there with more relish than ever before or since.

On the 25th we went on to Norrent Fontes, between Lillers and Aire, where we had a well earned fortnight's rest.

CHAPTER 11

Laventie

Norrent Fontes was a pleasant enough place, and seemed particularly so after our recent experiences; it was away from the noise of guns, and there were two respectably sized towns near, Lillers and Aire, so one saw a little civilisation.

New officers arrived at the end of October, notably Major Maitland, as second in command; Worsley came to my company; Gunnis took command of No. 3 Company, vice George Powell, who went home sick; and Captain Napoleon Vaughan had No. 4 in succession to Dowling, who had been wounded at Hohenzollern. Raymond Asquith joined the battalion at this time, so did Dick Stanhope, Alfred Yorke and John Hopley.

We did much training and drilling during this time, and everyone was taught how to throw a Mills bomb.

On October 28th we were to have been reviewed by His Majesty the King, but that morning His Majesty had that unfortunate accident that laid him up for so long, and the review was cancelled.

On November 8th we moved again to take our place in the line in the Neuve Chapelle—Laventie sector, a part of the line which had been famous early in the year, but which had since become fairly peaceful.

We had six days at La Gorgue, which was a fair-sized place joining on to Estaires, and which was the home of the brigade in reserve, the other two brigades being in the line.

On the 14th we first went into our new trenches. The Indians had just left them; they were in fair condition, but a lot of work was wanting on them. We started in the right sector just north of Neuve Chapelle.

The system was that one did two days in the front line, then two in farm houses at Riez Bailleul, and so on for twelve days, when one came back to reserve for six, either to La Gorgue or Merville, which was a little further back; and then back to the other sector (Laventie), and this system went on all that winter till we moved to Ypres. It was quite the quietest time we ever had in the war, and it was only because we stirred things up a bit that there was any liveliness at all. It was a pleasant change after the earlier part of the year; the mud was bad, but never got really out of hand; we worked incessantly on the trenches, and they were really excellent, particularly the Laventie sector.

While in this sector battalions used to billet in Laventie, only some 1,000 yards behind the front line, in complete safety; .the houses were nearly all intact, and the place full of inhabitants. I remember once marching to church with drums beating; that such things were possible so close showed how placid the Germans were at this time and place.

This winter the idea of raids into the enemy's lines first came into prominence, and there was always the chance of our being ordered to do a raid; so there was constant patrol work going on trying to find the best spot; as a matter of fact, the battalion never had to do a raid, though the 4th Battalion did one, also the 2nd Battalion Irish Guards.

In December we started having New-Army detachments attached to us for instruction, and we had elements of the Royal Welsh Fusiliers and the Wiltshire Yeomanry with us during the winter.

Stanhope took over command of No. 2 Company in the middle of December. Stewart getting a job at Havre.

We spent Christmas Day at Riez Bailleul, and cheerfully enough.

W. Parker joined the company at the end of December.

We had a battalion dinner on New Year's Eve in the town

hall at Merville, and we started the New Year off in the approved style.

On January 9th our next door neighbours, the 20th Division, did a gas attack at night, and it was rather an interesting sight.

On the 12th we had what was called a divisional demonstration, consisting of an artillery barrage and the firing of ten rounds rapid per man the whole length of the divisional front; it being all part of the idea of keeping up the offensive spirit, and also to find out exactly where the enemy would put down his counter barrage.

In the middle of the month Colonel Corry left us to command a brigade, and Colonel Jeffreys, who had just left the 2nd Battalion, also to command a brigade, came to us for a week while waiting for his vacancy, and until such time as our new commanding officer should arrive.

On the 18th Colonel Sergison Brooke, who had been brigade major of the 2nd Guards' Brigade, and afterwards on a corps staff, arrived to command.

On the 27th, which was the Kaiser's birthday, a day which always caused "wind" among the authorities, our artillery put down a barrage at 5 a.m., as a damper to the German in case he should have planned a visit to our trenches as part of the All Highest's birthday celebrations.

On February 5th the battalion was called upon to give an exhibition of drill before an eminent Russian statesman (I forget his name) who was visiting the Western front; he was not a soldier, so I doubt if he knew our bad points from our good!

On the 10th Ralph Parker, of No. 4 Company, was wounded by one of our own bayonets jumping into a trench on returning from a patrol, and I was lent to that company under Napoleon Vaughan.

On the 16th February our long tenure of this piece of country came to an end, and the 9th Battalion Royal Welsh Fusiliers (58th Brigade, 19th Division) relieved us; and we returned to La Gorgue preparatory to going north, and so our winter campaign came to an end. It had not been particularly eventful; but we were at it all the time, always more or less in danger, and the cold and wet was trying at times, but, as I have said before, it was our mildest job.

CHAPTER 12

Ypres, 1916

On February 19th we started north, stopping *en route* at Eecke, and then on to Poperinghe.

On March 5th we left for training at Calais, each brigade going there in turn; we were under canvas, and it was none too warm.

Sir Douglas Haig inspected the 2nd Guards' Brigade on the 6th.

On the 12th we had a race meeting on the sands.

Hard training in the morning, and football, etc., in the afternoon filled up our time till we left on the 17th *en route* for Ypres.

We stopped on the way at Oudezeele, a small village at the foot of Cassel Hill, which was the most prominent feature of that part of the country, and where General Plumer had his headquarters.

On the 20th we left for Poperinghe, where we were in reserve for six days. Poperinghe had been a good deal knocked about since I last saw it, early in 1915, but was still a good town, with plenty of inhabitants; one rather expected a shell to arrive any moment, but it was marvellous how little it got shelled, except round the railway station.

On the 26th the battalion left for that dreaded place, Ypres; the Salient always had a nasty reputation, and well it deserved it; however quiet things were elsewhere, there was always something doing here. Merely holding the salient cost us thousands of casualties, but the moral effect of withdrawing would have been bad, and so we had to endure that horrible "Salient feeling," and put up with those shells that seemed to come almost from behind, and all the hundred and one minor horrors of this hell on earth.

And so it was with no light heart that we took up our place in the Ypres Salient; we knew what to expect, and we got it.

Well, we got up to Ypres all right. Most of the battalion were actually in the town, in cellars; there were a few houses in which one could have lived on the ground floor, but it wasn't really safe, as shells were flying about all the time; I was sent a mile or two further on to hold an earthwork called the Potijde defences with two platoons. Potijde was a small village with a *château* which furnished the battalion H.Q. for the front line battalion, in this case the 1st Battalion Scots Guards.

We soon got a taste of the charms of the Salient; the Germans had all the observation there, and must have had very highly trained troops opposite us; our slightest movement was detected and sniped, not with rifles, but with 4.2 howitzers! Here we were some 1,500 yards from the front, but one couldn't move a yard by day; I remember seeing an optimistic officer, evidently returning from leave, marching gaily up the Potijde road with his servant behind carrying his valise, and the Germans as near as anything got them with the opening shot; after that they proceeded with more caution. One of my men jumped out of the trench for one moment to fetch something in, and quick as lightning came a 4.2 shell, missing him by inches.

I didn't enjoy this place much, especially as it was a reserve position, and our next move was to be forward. However, after two nights, Worsley relieved me, and I joined the rest of the company in Ypres; they had a beautifully furnished cellar, and I got a good rest there before going up to the front line.

Ypres was a very different place to what it had been when I last saw it in April, 1915; all the civilians had gone; there hadn't been many there since the gas attack in May. Every house had been hit, the part round the square was completely destroyed;

the western-most part had got off lightest, and the prison was still more or less a building. Shells fell in the town every day, especially at dusk, when it was hoped to catch our transport coming up.

We had quite a lot of troops there, but they all lived below ground, except for a few adventurous souls who used to go on souvenir hunting expeditions. I used to get in for some of these, but was always glad to return to earth again.

We first started wearing the steel helmet at this time, and very heavy and uncomfortable it felt at first.

On the night 30th–31st March, a night never to be forgotten, though it produced no actual battle movement, the battalion moved to relieve the Scots Guards. There had been heavy firing all day, and at one time the relief was postponed, as it was thought an attack was imminent. However, the shelling ceased, only to start again just as we were reaching our position.

My company was to be in support in the line just in front of Potijde, with No. 1 on our right and 3 and 4 in the front line. We found the Scots Guards in a baddish way; they had endured a terrible shelling all the afternoon, and the trenches were full of their dead. The company we relieved was commanded by Sir Ian Colquhoun, a man of unusual fearlessness; he had taken up a position under the parapet, and he told us that that particular portion had remained intact all day, and he advised us to make it our H.Q., which we did.

The shelling at this time was severe, but worse in front, and our front companies found no trenches to hold; they had all been blown in, and very few men to relieve; they had all been killed or wounded: but they took up a position among the shell holes, and started reconsolidating.

The shelling eased off a bit, and eventually we only got a quarter of an hour intense in every hour, starting punctually at the hour, so we knew what and when to expect it. At 4.15 it stopped altogether, and our guns, which had been strangely silent, began and fired hard for an hour and a half. Their previous silence was explained by the fact that they were waiting to deal with the attack which certainly seemed to be coming; all the gunners were "standing to" ready all night.

It was a bad night, and we wondered if it was a typical Ypres night or merely a welcome from the Boche; mercifully it proved to be the latter, and we found after that the welcome had been extended to the whole of the Guards' divisional front. We had many dirty nights in the Salient later on, but never one as dirty as this one.

We spent the quieter moments digging out the trenches, and getting the dead and wounded Scotsmen away. We had a good many casualties, too; I had been ordered to bring the ration party up in the rear of the company, and on getting to the trench I found most of my platoon lying in the road groaning; a big shell had pitched right in the middle of them just as they were going to turn into the trench, and all three sergeants of the platoon were hit, one eventually dying.

Two days later we moved to the front line; this was still in a dreadful state, though our No. 4 Company, under Alfred Yorke, had done wonders, and it, at any rate, looked like a defensive position. It was very wet and muddy, and altogether bad.

Next morning, while I was having a bit of rest in the so-called dugout, a piece of corrugated iron stretched across sandbags, what was known as the Pilkem gun started firing; it fired at us enfilade, and slap down our trench; the first shot missed our H.Q. by inches, and made an enormous hole exactly where Dick Stanhope had been having a wash a few minutes before, and where he had left his soap and towels. On hearing the explosion he came rushing back to rescue, not his young officers, but his towel!—or so we always told him afterwards. He was wonderful all this time, quite unconcerned, and seemed to be enjoying it all; he and Worsley were the other officers in the company; they were both killed later in the war.

The system in this part of the line was sixteen days in the forwards area (two in front and two in Ypres, and so on), and then eight in reserve at Poperinghe, and then back into the next sector. Thus we stayed up till the 11th, when the 1st Brigade relieved us.

We had had a fairly quiet time after our start, and had been busy draining and digging out the trenches, and had got them more or less inhabitable again.

Just before we were relieved by the 3rd Battalion Coldstream, trouble broke out on our left, the Germans doing a daylight raid on the 20th Division under a very heavy barrage of trench mortars and artillery. Things looked rather bad there, and one wondered if it would spread to us, but by dark all was quiet, and our relief went off peacefully enough.

We had eight days in Poperinghe, and enjoyed them thoroughly; what those periods of rest meant to us in those days no one can imagine who has not had a bad time in the front line; they were invaluable, and just kept one going. There were cinemas and pierrot shows to go to; among the latter the 6th Division "Fancies" were quite excellent, and played to a crowded house every evening; then we used to have dinner parties, and generally tried to be as civilised as we could.

On the 19th we were due to return to Ypres. Just before we were to leave Poperinghe a heavy bombardment started in front, and the relief was postponed for a time, but we "stood by" ready for any emergency. Late at night we went off, and reached our cellars in Ypres without calamity. The noise of the evening of the 19th was the Germans doing an attack at the junction of the Guards' Division and the 6th Division at Wieltje; our 4th Battalion and the 2nd Battalion Scots Guards were involved in this, and the net result was that the 6th Division lost a small piece of trench, which, however, they regained by a counter attack on the night of the 22nd-23rd.

On the 24th the battalion relieved the 1st Battalion Scots Guards in the front system, my company being in reserve in the canal bank. This bank was lined with dugouts of varying sizes and importance; Brigadiers lived there, sapper officers, gunners, every type of front line soldier; it was a perfect hub.

The 2nd Brigade held the line till the 5th May; there were a few excitements during that time; the Germans came up and bombed our company's front one night, and there was a good deal of noise, and a few people were hit, but it didn't come to much. On the 3rd the 3rd Guards' Brigade on our right blew up a mine at Railway Wood, and a good deal of shelling resulted. Then Brigadier-General Heyworth was killed a day or two after, being sniped on his way up to the front line.

On the 9th Stanhope went on leave, and for the first time I was entrusted with the command of the company.

We were back again at Ypres on the 12th, and in the front lines at Potijze on the 16th. It was much quieter during this tour of duty, and I remember bragging to the commanding officer (Colonel Brooke) that not a German shell had come into our trench during the whole time we were there.

On the 21st the Guards' Division was relieved by the 20th Division; we were relieved by the 12th Battalion Rifle Brigade.

We had managed to put in a lot of work on the trenches, and the officer of the rifle brigade, who relieved me, said he had no idea such good trenches existed or could exist in the Ypres Salient.

The division went back to rest for a month, and I went on ten days' leave. I went off straight from the front line, and a machine gun shot at me all the way down the road from Potijze to Ypres, and I remember wondering if the Germans were going to stop my leave!

I rejoined the battalion on the 3rd June at Volkeringhove, where they were still resting. On the 4th we had the annual Eton dinner, there being thirty or forty of us from the 2nd Guards' Brigade, presided over by Brigadier-General John Ponsonby. This took place in the school, and may claim to have been a success.

During this rest we were to practise a projected attack on the Pilkem ridge; the possession of this ridge by the Germans was always a trouble to us, and it was thought the moment had arrived to dispossess them of it. Thus we dug an exact copy of the trenches there, and put in imitation farms, etc., and practised every day this rather intricate problem. As a matter of fact, this attack didn't come off till a year later (July 31st, 1917).

Our month's rest was nearing its allotted end, and we were

getting used to the idea of returning to the Salient and capturing the Pilkem ridge on the north side; but on the 14th we were suddenly sent for to the south side of the Salient, and we left in lorries post haste to Vlamertinghe.

CHAPTER 13

Ypres, 1916 Continued

The trouble this time was on the Canadian front at Hooge; the Germans had attacked strongly from Hooge on the north to about Hill 60 on the south, including in this the famous Sanctuary Wood; they gained some ground, and though a comparatively small battle, it had been particularly fierce, and the shelling had been terrific; the Canadians later carried out a fine counter-attack and regained all the important points lost.

The position was obscure to us when we started off in our lorries, and we didn't know what we might, be called on to do. However, we had a night at Vlamertinghe in a camp, and it then transpired that the 2nd Guards' Brigade was to relieve the Canadian Division for a week, so that they might have a chance of reorganising themselves. I gather the Guards' Division volunteered to send help, and I remember, although the task wasn't any too pleasant, we felt gratified at being able to lend a helping hand to our Colonial friends for whose fighting abilities we had such great admiration.

On the 15th the battalion moved forward to the south side of Ypres; three companies were round the Zillebeke Bund (or lake), and the remaining one in the remains of the cavalry barracks in Ypres; my company was the latter. Next night there were constant alarms, there was terrific artillery fire all night, and several rumoured gas attacks; the company was "standing to" practically all night.

It was a wonderful night, and the shelling was a wonderful

sight, looked at from the ramparts of the city, a semi-circular line of flame from one end of the salient to the other. Nothing tangible resulted, and there was no attack.

On the 18th we went into the front line in Sanctuary Wood, just in front of Zillebeke village. Sanctuary Wood was a dreadful place, a perfect shambles; dead Germans and dead Canadians everywhere; the trenches were only about three feet deep, and it was well-nigh impossible to dig deeper owing to the bodies and debris. There was one particularly gruesome dugout where some half-dozen Germans were sitting, just opening a parcel; they were all unwounded, but all dead, apparently gassed during our counter attack.

I was put in the front line of all with two platoons, with Heasman under me; Stanhope and Thrupp were behind with the rest of the company. I shall never forget Sanctuary Wood if I live to the age of Methusaleh. It was midsummer, and light for nineteen out of the twenty-four hours; thus for nineteen hours per day one couldn't move a muscle, but just lay at the bottom of the trench, getting shelled by 5.9 shells which traversed the trench at intervals; if it hadn't been for two bottles of port which we had contrived to bring up with us, I think our morale would have entirely departed. The trench was stuffed full of men, and we were all sitting in each other's laps. I luckily found myself next to the company wag, one Tonge, whose wit became more intense as the situation grew worse; men like him were invaluable at times like this.

So we lived for three days; at night everyone got up and walked about No-man's-land to stretch their legs. The German infantry were very quiet, but their gunners were all too active. Herbert Eaton, in the next company (No. 1) was blown up by a shell here, and was lucky not to be worse hit.

On the 21st the Canadians returned, and the 42nd Canadian Highlanders relieved us.

After this we returned to our sector, in the northern half, where we were due to relieve the 1st Guards' Brigade. However, we were rested till the 28th.

At this time the great offensive down south, which everyone had been thinking of, if not exactly talking about, for a long time, was getting ready to start; and we were told that there would be "an intense fortnight" in the Ypres Salient as a diversion to prevent reinforcements being sent to the Somme.

An all-day bombardment was fixed for the 1st of July, and a raid by the 2nd Battalion Irish Guards for the 2nd, various minor demonstrations were to follow.

We got into the front line on the 30th. We were now the left of the British army, with the French next to us.

Next morning we got ready for the big bombardment. I think we expected one continuous roar all day long, so it was a trifle disappointing, and although a good quantity of stuff was despatched to Germany, it didn't strike one as being a particularly noteworthy display; the Germans retaliated, of course, and we had a pretty lively time dodging shells.

The Irish Guards' raid was a more important operation. I think its object was chiefly to keep the Germans alert on our front and thus help the big battle; also, prisoners were required for identification purposes. The raid was to be carried out by about a platoon of volunteers under Lieutenant Francis Pym. who was a particular friend of mine, with whom I had shared rooms before the war. The raid took place just as it was getting dark, under cover of a hurricane bombardment; from all accounts it was successful, and after a confused fight in the German trench, some prisoners were brought back to our lines, but the Irishmen suffered heavily from the shell-fire, and had heavy casualties, including Pym, whose exact fate remains a mystery to this day; he was seen to be doing magnificently in the German trench, and left with the party at the conclusion of the operation, but was never seen again, nor was any sign or trace of him ever discovered.

We were just on the left of all this, and got in for the retaliating shelling, an hour of the best. It was dark, so the Germans had no observation, and luckily their shooting was a bit wild, and we had no casualties, though it was a miracle.

We were in and out of the front line till the 14th, when the 3rd Brigade relieved us. Nothing much happened—the usual shellings and the usual weariness. On the evening of the 12th the Germans shelled the canal bridges heavily, and one thought for a time that they were trying to cut our communications with the other side, preparatory to raiding us, but nothing happened.

We returned then to camp in what was known as A. 30 Forest, owing to its position on the map; it was some three miles east of Poperinghe. Here we rested, drilled and played cricket, etc.

On the 21st we had a Brigade cricket match, Old Etonians v. The World, on a matting wicket, with occasional shells bursting round; the former won fairly easily.

That evening the brigadier (General Ponsonby) gave a party at his hut to the officers of his brigade; the Scots Guards' band played, and the place was lit up with lanterns, and the refreshments were good and plentiful; we danced with each other vigorously, and altogether it was a pleasant diversion from the ordinary sort of life.

On the 23rd we should have gone up to relieve the 1st Brigade, but it was cancelled, and rumours of a move south became insistent.

It had been rather a disappointment to think that the Battle of the Somme should be fought without the brigade of Guards taking part in it, the only big battle in the war missed by them; so when we were told we were going off to take part in this battle, we were pleased, and anyway, a change from the Salient seemed a good idea.

So on the 25th July we bid a temporary goodbye to the Salient (we were destined to return next year), and went to Volkeringhove to concentrate for the movement south.

CHAPTER 14.

The Battle of the Somme

We stayed at Volkeringhove till the 29th, during which time we trained, and also had battalion sports.

The battalion was in very good fettle now, and keen to have another proper fight with the Germans after so many months of trench warfare.

There had been a few changes among the officers, and the companies, when we left for the Somme, were commanded by (1) Wolridge Gordon, (2) Stanhope, (3) Hopley, (4) Mackenzie. Colonel Brooke still commanded, with Major Rasch second in command, and Oliver Lyttleton adjutant.

We entrained on the 20th at Bollezeele, and travelling all night, arrived at a little place called Petit Houin, not far from St. Pol. Here we detrained and marched some way to La Souich; it was a very hot day, and the march was somewhat trying. La Souich is a pretty little place close to Doullens.

We did not stay there long, leaving for the forward area on the 1st, having dinners and bathing at Loucheux *en route*. We went on in lorries to the Courcelles au Bois area; this place was some three miles from the front line.

For some time the authorities seemed undecided where to use us, and we moved about from place to place doing various jobs until we finally settled more or less on the British right wing.

We bivouacked at Courcelles; the weather was frightfully hot, and there was practically no shade, so we weren't very comfortable there.

We used to go up to the front line every night to dig trenches for the 20th Division, the idea then being that we should eventually take over that part of the line and attack from there. This was the extreme left of the original attack on July 1st, and here the attack had failed.

We continued digging up till the 6th, and really made some extraordinarily fine trenches for the other division to live in; they, I think, were amazed at the work done in so short a time. We got shelled from time to time, but the worst danger was from trench mortars, which were rather active just here. Their bombs were particularly annoying, as they can't be heard coming, and they explode with unusual force.

It was tiring work, as it was so hot in the day, and the flies so tiresome that one couldn't sleep much; the actual trenches we worked on were near La Signy Farm, and just in front of Colincamps Village.

On the 7th we left to camp in the Bois de Warnimont, a big wood some four miles further back.

We expected to be here some time, but on the 9th the Brigade was ordered forward again to take over the trenches at Beaumont Hamel, south of where we had been. The battalion was in reserve to start with, first at Beaussart and then at Bertrancourt, just behind; on the 13th we left for the front line, passing *en route* through the villages of Mailly-Maillet and Auchenvillers, both rather shelly places.

The Beaumont Hamel trenches were wonderfully good, with deep dugouts, luxuries unheard of at Ypres, and altogether we seemed to be in for a fairly peaceful time there, the only difficulty being finding one's way about in the maze of trenches.

Next day we were told there was to be a gas attack on our front; gas was already installed on our front; if the wind was favourable we were to let it off. The place swarmed with gas experts from various H.Q.'s in the rear. I'm afraid we didn't welcome them much, as we knew the only result we should see of the gas attack would be a good sound shelling from the Germans. Everything was arranged, and we made gas-proof dugouts in case there were any accidents to our men in letting it off; there was to be an accompanying bombardment of some intensity.

At the critical moment the wind changed, and the show was off, except for the bombardment, which took place as advertised. We got some back, of course, but it wasn't very alarming.

Next day we were suddenly told we were to be relieved by another division; so the 8th Batt. Bedford Regiment came up in the evening of the 15th, and we left to bivouac near Mailly-Maillet.

We were not destined to stay there long, as next day we moved back to Bertrancourt, and the day after to Sailly-au-Bois, which was the next village to Courcelles, where we had been before.

The 2nd Guards' Brigade had been ordered to hold the front here for four days, but as we had done more work than the other battalions up to date, it didn't take us to go further up than Sailly, which was about three miles behind the front; but all the same it was not exactly a bed of roses there, and we very narrowly missed what would have been perhaps our worst calamity of the war from the officer point of view.

Our bivouac was situated just west of the ruined village of Sailly and just behind us was a battery of heavy guns; both of these were favourite targets for the German gunners, and it soon became apparent that we had been given a most unhealthy place to live in. All the officers messed together under a large tarpaulin sheet, and we had all assembled for lunch on our first day there, when a large shell was heard approaching. It just skimmed over the tarpaulin and burst a few yards over; just those few yards shorter, and it would have left the 3rd Battalion officerless. This shell was the first of a hurricane bombardment of our bivouac, and the whole battalion had to clear out for some time till peace was restored. The same thing happened that evening about 8 p.m., so we were ordered to change our position, and we went into a valley a few hundred yards off, where we remained un-molested, and had the pleasure of watching our old home being daily shelled.

65

It is most unpleasant being shelled in a camp or bivouac, and there was much consternation in the officers' mess, particularly to one newly joined ensign with some culinary attainments who was busy cooking a kidney omelette at the time; he was put to flight in his shirt-sleeves, and the omelette left to spoil.

On the 20th we were the unwilling witnesses of the tragedy of Basil Hallam. We were amusing ourselves that evening playing rounders, when we saw an observation balloon approaching rapidly from the west, apparently broken away from its moorings. It was making straight for the German lines. Next we saw a dark object fall from the balloon; it didn't seem to us at the time that it was a man, but so it proved to be; the body fell just in the village of Sailly-au-Bois, and was found to be Hallam, who had been in charge of a Balloon Section at Couin just behind us; he had apparently had some trouble with his parachute; his sergeant, more lucky, reached the ground safely.

On the 21st we got on the move again, going to a hut camp at Bus-les-Artois. After two nights there we were ordered south, to the right of the British line, going via Ampliers and Naours, both in the Doullens district, and then by train *via* Amiens to Morlancourt, where we stayed for about a fortnight training.

Morlancourt was a long, straggling village, and remarkably dirty; troops had been there continuously, and had never bothered to clean up before moving; result, flies everywhere and general unhealthiness. But it wasn't a bad place once we got settled in, and we were allowed in Amiens occasionally, and on the whole we rather enjoyed ourselves there, and it was well that we did so, as for so many of us it was our last experience of this world; for that dread 15th of September was close upon us, a day when the Brigade of Guards suffered as it had never suffered before, and, please God, may never suffer again.

Thus, Morlancourt remains a pleasant memory.

Since we left the Ypres Salient, new officers had arrived, among them Hirst (who had been wounded at Hohenzollern Redoubt), St. J. Williams, Stainton, Cornish, Gardiner, Penfold, and Cassy; the company commanders remained the same.

We made particular friends here with the officers of the 2nd Guards' Brigade Machine Gun Company; there were nine of them altogether, and not one of them escaped on the 15th, seven being killed and two wounded; a nicer lot of fellows were never to be found.

We practised attacking behind a creeping barrage here, the drums being used to represent shells bursting. The field days happened daily till the 9th, when we moved up to a big valley known as Happy Valley.

The tanks made their first appearance here, and were parked together in a field, and caused much excitement.

The part the brigade was to play in the great battle now at last became apparent; desultory fights had been going on all the time, the Irish troops doing especially gallant deeds and suffering heavily. Guillemont village took a lot of capturing, and for about a week the battle raged for its possession; the carnage was terrible, and we got an inkling of what might happen to us when we saw battalions marching back to rest, the strength of small companies.

It was on the 9th September, if I remember right, that Ginchy was captured, the Irish Division being relieved by the 3rd Guards' Brigade in the evening; the village had not been completely cleared, and the 3rd Brigade had work to do on their way up to relieve.

The 3rd Brigade (to be in reserve for the big battle) held the line till the 13th, and had a hard time, the Germans counter attacking several times, but to no purpose, the 1st Battalion and the Welsh Guards particularly distinguishing themselves.

The 2nd Guards' Brigade had meantime moved forward to the Carnoy area, and on the 13th the 1st Battalion Scots and 2nd Battalion Irish Guards relieved the front line, the 1st Battalion Coldstream and ourselves, who were to be in the front line of the attack, remaining in bivouacs at Carnoy.

We left one officer per company out of the attack, and it fell to my lot to be left out, the others being Bowes-Lyon, Ralph Parker (both killed later in the war), and Neville; added to these were Guy Rasch, the second in command, and Duquenoy, the transport officer. We were left behind at Happy Valley when the battalion left for Carnoy, but we used to ride up and see them every day. On the morning of the 15th the "*embusqués*," as we called ourselves, moved up in front of Carnoy village ready to go up to the fight if required.

The battalion left Carnoy bivouac on the evening of the 14th, and it wasn't pleasant watching them go off.

The attack was timed for 6.20 next morning, and proved one of the most difficult but gallant affairs of the whole war. Tanks were used for the first time; there was no preliminary bombardment as at Loos and elsewhere, and all was quiet till zero hour.

The attack on the Guards' Division front was entrusted to the 1st and 2nd Guards' Brigades, with the 2nd and 3rd Battalions Coldstream of the 1st Brigade, and the 1st Battalion Coldstream and ourselves in the front line, the supporting battalions, *i.e.*, 2nd Batt. Grenadier, 1st Batt. Irish, the 1st Batt. Scots Guards, and 2nd Batt. Irish were quite close behind, and became involved almost at once.

It was a terrible fight; the 6th Division on our immediate right were held up by machine gun fire from an earthwork known as the Quadrilateral, and didn't advance at all; this left our right in the air, but did not stop our advance, nor did the storm of machine gun bullets which greeted the attack; the final objective was Les Boeufs Village, but it was only possible, owing to the exposed flank, to reach the second objective, short of the village.

I was not present myself, as I have already explained, so have no personal impressions of this day, but I gather that it was quite the worst battle of the war. The division is reputed to have had 6,000 casualties in these few hours' fighting, all battalions losing about sixty *per cent,* of their effectives, and some eighty or ninety *per cent,* of their officers. We (the 3rd Battalion) lost some 380 men and eighteen out of the twenty-one officers.

The 3rd Guards' Brigade, originally in reserve, was ordered to form a defensive flank on our right. We had ten officers killed—

Allan Mackenzie, Dick Stanhope, Wynne, Gunnis, Gardiner, Stainton, E. Worsley, Raymond Asquith, Jackson, and Logan, the medical officer—and eight wounded—Colonel Brooke, Williams, Thrupp, Cornish, Whitehead, Champneys, John Hopley, and Cassy; the only ones to escape untouched being Wolridge Gordon, Lyttelton, and Hirst. The latter was at first reported killed, and I remember sending his kit away from the tent allotted to him, when he turned up with the remains of the company and none the worse.

As to my part in the battle, our little party remained near Carnoy, hearing the most awful rumours of disaster, and only too true generally. A steady gloom descended on us. and I doubt if I have ever spent a more miserable day.

The battalion was relieved on the night of the 16th-17th, and came back to a camp at a place called the citadel, not far from Fricourt. It was sad work seeing them come in with ranks so depleted; it had been such a magnificent battalion, everyone so keen, and trained up to a "T."

Next day, Sunday, the remains of the brigade paraded together for church parade, and later the brigadier (John Ponsonby) saw the battalion and thanked them for what they had done.

Reinforcements arrived, and we became a full battalion once more; Eric Anson (wounded at Loos) returned, and Aubrey Hall arrived.

Before long it was rumoured that we were "for it" again, and it transpired that there was to be another attack to capture Les Boeufs on the 25th.

On the 20th we moved up to Carnoy again to a bivouac which was rather apt to be shelled by long range naval guns.

In this battle the 1st and 3rd Brigades were in the front lines, and our brigade in reserve; the battalion was in corps reserve, and might be used on any part of the 14th Corps front. As it turned out, the battle was a complete success, and the 2nd Brigade was not used at all. Les Boeufs was captured, as also was Morval (by the 5th Division).

Next day we moved up to Trones Wood, and the Scots Guards

went up to relieve at Les Boeufs.

On the 27th my company had the unpleasant job of burying the dead. We had to bury the dead lying out in the open in front of Ginchy, at the spot where the attack on the 15th had started; the weather was hot, and they had been lying out twelve days, and were almost all turned jet black; we buried that morning some 200 men, rather more Germans than English; it was a nasty fatigue, and I won't dwell more on it.

On the 28th we relieved the Scots Guards in front of Les Boeufs; we had a long and weary walk up there in pitch darkness, falling into shell holes, etc., and shelled most of the way, but we got there, and found our company had to hold a sunken road; this road seemed a perfect inferno—shells everywhere.

I had previously been detailed for a patrol. Our job was to advance, in conjunction with patrols from the whole division, 750 yards towards the enemy, dig in there, and stay next day there, when the remainder of the battalion would come up and consolidate.

Well, it didn't sound a very pretty job to me, and I remember thinking my number was probably up. But as I had escaped the two preceding battles it was certainly my turn for something dirty.

I had twelve men and a sergeant; the latter I selected specially as the bravest and most efficient in the company, Sergeant A. E. Smith, a man who stood out by himself either on parade or in the trenches. So off we went, along another sunken road leading to Le Transloy, Sergeant Smith counting the paces as we went. We proceeded with due precautions, with point and flankers out; there was no opposition, and on completing our 750 paces we lined out and proceeded to dig. We were promptly shelled by our own side, and I decided to go fifty yards back, where we luckily found some partly dug rifle pits which we proceeded to improve; it was very hard work, the ground being like iron, and we had no picks with us. I fixed on my H.Q. in the bank of the sunken road, and put my servant on to scooping out a little place in the bank for us to spend next day in, and if possible sleep in.

It was a nightmare, that night; German shells were falling just over us all night long, our own from the other direction doing the same; the whole fury of the battle seemed to concentrate on us.

However, we got on with the work pretty well, and by dawn had made ourselves a place to live in. I had just given the order to resume "day conditions," or, in other words, get into the trench and settle down for the day, when our own field guns started a terrific and most accurate bombardment of our new position. I was slightly wounded, as were two of the men. The thing looked awkward; there was a thick mist, and no immediate way of communicating with the battery firing on us, even if we knew which it was. I sent a man back to the company H.Q. to report the position, and then returned to my place in the sunken road to see the extent of the damage done to myself.

The shelling stopped and all was quiet, except for German shells falling on our main lines, so I decided I would go and have my wound looked at and then return; so off I went, back to Company H.Q., with my servant, as near as anything being picked off by a German shell *en route*.

On arriving at C.H.Q. I first drank a whole bottle of beer, and then had my wound, which was quite small, tied up: I was told to go back to the battalion aid post, as it was thought there was a piece of shell still in. Before I left, a belated message arrived ordering my patrol to come in about three hours before.

On my way down I met the commanding officer (Lieutenant-Colonel Thorne, who had succeeded Colonel Brooke) with some staff officers, and explained the situation to him; it appeared our gunners had been ordered to barrage a certain ridge, but had got on to the wrong one, thus disturbing us.

I went on by various stages to hospital at Le Touquet. stopping *en route* at a C.C.S. at Bray-sur-Somme. My wound was nothing really, and soon healed, and on October 6th I left hospital fit, and was sent to the Guards' Division Base Depôt at Havre.

Here I had a very pleasant rest, the base, under the régime of Colonel Royds, Scots Guards, being one of the pleasantest places on the Western front, and a very Heaven after the Somme battlefield.

I got some leave during this time, and eventually rejoined the battalion on the 24th November at the citadel, Fricourt.

CHAPTER 15

Sailly, Saillisel and the St. Pierre Vaast

I found that the battalion had just returned to the battle area from resting behind at Heucourt.

I had not missed any fighting or trench work. I was greeted by the remark that they had been having a wonderful time, but that now we looked like having a pretty moderate one.

The battalion was a good deal changed, and the company commanders were all different, John Craigie commanding No. 1, Ivor Rose No. 2, Dowling No. 3, and Ralph Parker No. 4. I went back to my old company, No. 2, the other officers there being Hirst and Hall.

The citadel was a cheerless place, all mud, and it was terribly cold. We slept in tents and messed in a tin shed.

The Germans had been giving trouble on the right of our line at Sailly Saillisel, where we joined on to the French, and our job was to relieve the French at that place, and just hold the line. So, *en route* for Sailly, we left for Abre Forchée camp on the 27th; this was a French hut camp close to Bray, and quite good.

We had just arrived there when I was ordered off to the 14th Corps Lewis Gun School at Meaulte. So I went off there, and finding our 1st Battalion billeted in the village, got leave to live with them instead of at the school among complete strangers, and I became the guest of Wilfred Dashwood during my five days' course.

The Lewis gun rather defeated me, but I managed to make them think I knew something about it, and left without loss of name or reputation.

I rejoined the battalion on December 2nd. They had meanwhile moved up to the front line at Sailly Saillisel. My company was in reserve at Haie Wood in dugouts, moderately safe and comfortable; the trenches in front were terribly bad, and there was an awful lot of work to be done on them before they became either inhabitable or defensible. Hence fatigues and working parties were innumerable.

The Germans were pretty active, and there were a lot of shells about; they had raided the French just as we got up to relieve them, and they pinched a machine gun; but luckily the man carrying it was shot on his way home, and we were able to recover the gun and give it back to the French. The French blamed us for the original occurrence, and said we made too much noise coming up, thus rousing the Germans' curiosity; they were rather cross with us really, but the return of their lost gun restored the situation!

But to return to the trenches; the reserve company used to work all night carrying wire and stakes, etc., up to the front; tiring work in the mud and dark, and not altogether safe; they put a shell into the tail end of the company one night on our way home; I was marching in the rear of the company, and it killed the men just in front of me and wounded two others. It was an unpleasant incident; perhaps it was luck it didn't happen more frequently.

On the 5th the reserve company was relieved by the 1st Batt. Scots Guards, the rest of the battalion by our 4th Battalion.

The division was now divided into two groups, the idea being that by that system one got shorter hours of duty in the front line, which, owing to the awful condition of the trenches, was essential. On the other hand, under the new system one always seemed to be on the move, never more than three days in one place.

Our group consisted of the 1st, 3rd and 4th Battalions Grenadier Guards, the 1st and 2nd Battalions Scots Guards, and the Welsh Guards, and was responsible for the left half of the divisional front.

On relief, we went to Maltzhorn Farm camp near Trones Wood; we had a shelly march back, taking three hours or more altogether. After three hours solid marching one felt one ought to be out of range, but it was not so, and we got some going through Guillemont village, and more on arriving at the camp. The camp was filthy, and we only had time to remove some of the filth when we had to move back to Bronfay Farm camp, near the Plateau railhead.

This was on the 6th, and on the 9th we moved forward once more to Bouleaux Wood in reserve. Here we lived very crowded in long dugouts; we were surrounded with our guns, which were continually being shelled, so it was a warmish corner.

We did wiring fatigues here; the C.O., to spur us on in our unpleasant task, offered a prize to the company which completed its allotted task first; the prize took the form of beer, if I remember right; the result was that all the companies claimed to have won so the whole battalion got beer! Anyhow, some very good wiring was done.

On the night of the 11th-12th we relieved our 1st Battalion in the front lines. It took Nos. 1, 2 and 3 Companies for the firing line this time; Hirst was now commanding No. 2, Rose having gone to command the new Works Battalion; I was the only other officer in the company; we shared a deep dugout with No. 3 Company's officers, consisting of Dowling, Neville, and, I think, Holbech, who had just joined.

I had seen bad trenches before, but Sailly Saillisel beat all known records. Mud of such consistency probably never existed elsewhere. Men were literally glued to their positions. To get along the company front was a physical impossibility; one tried, of course, but after having stuck several times, generally gave it up as a bad job. Added to this, it was bitterly cold and raining hard. Water poured down our dugout steps, and we looked like being flooded out; continuous feats of engineering prevented this; the men were in a dreadful condition, practically speechless with cold, and unable to move. After that first night and day one really began to wonder what would happen, and I really thought we should have no men left alive after another night, and moreover, we were not to be relieved till the fourth night. The men were, as ever, wonderful, and they saw the thing through. I doubt if any men had to put up with a sterner test of physical endurance in the whole war.

We had a good deal of trouble coming up to relieve, men continually getting stuck and having to be pulled out; confusion became worse confounded by a Verey light going up just as we were nearing the front line, and by some misguided person, said to be an officer of another company, ordering one of our platoons to jump into a communication trench to avoid being seen. I arrived with the rear of the company, and found them floundering in the morass, and it took a considerable time to get them all out. Many men lost their gum boots and arrived barefooted in the trenches.

During the second night the company commanders decided that they would ask if they might be relieved twenty-four hours sooner, as things seemed to be becoming so desperate for the men; this request was refused, and eventually it was decided to hold the line only in posts, choosing the dryer parts of the trench for inhabitation; this system worked well, and was, I believe, kept up all the rest of our time there.

I had the shock of my life in the early morning of the 13th; a terrific barrage had started just on our left, rain was pouring down, the trench was getting rapidly worse, and the company was standing to arms in case the barrage meant anything. Things had never looked so black, when a figure loomed up in the darkness; it was the assistant adjutant (Frank Eaton) come up from B.H.Q. with orders for me to proceed immediately to Havre as an instructor for two months at the Central Training School there.

My relief at leaving this scene of desolation can be imagined, but one didn't feel too well about deserting the sinking ship. I went off in the morning with my servant and a sergeant, also due for Havre; we had a long and weary walk through the mud, and arrived exhausted at our transport, lines, where we endeavoured to make ourselves presentable for our return to civilisation.

The division in those days kept two officers at Havre instructing in the school; it was a two months' job, and was by way of being a rest from the line; one's work there was to put all drafts through various tests before they went up to join their units. Bowes-Lyon had been going for us, but went sick at the last moment, so I got the job instead.

While doing this job I lived at the Guards' Division Base Depôt, of whose excellence I have already spoken in a previous chapter. I do not intend to dwell long on these two months.

It was very cold there—the wine even used to freeze in the mess; what it must have been like in the line then I tremble to think, Major Mitchell, a grenadier, was in charge of the school; at first I was put to look after the drill, later bayonet fighting; I cannot say I enjoyed the work much, and I was glad enough when my time came to return to the battalion, which I did on Feb. 21st.

I found them at Billon Farm, near Maricourt, in Divisional Reserve. Lieutenant-Colonel Thorne was still commanding, with Major Rasch as second in command; Frank Eaton was adjutant, and companies were commanded as follows: (1) John Cragie, (2) Hirst, (3) Neville, (4) Parker. I went back to No. 2, as before, the other officers being Holbech and Allan Adair, who had only recently joined.

We trained for about a week at Billon Farm, and then moved up to Maurepas in Brigade Reserve on the 26th, leaving next day for the front lines. No. 2 Company was in reserve trenches behind Rancourt. Next morning, at dawn, the 29th Division, on our left, did a small attack at Sailly Saillisel, and our artillery carried out a sympathetic bombardment.

It was a wonderful noise; there is something most awe-aspiring in the start of a barrage. It is still dark, and all is dead quiet, when suddenly two or three guns, who have synchronised badly, fire, followed by the full chorus, and hell is let loose. That morning it didn't last long, but we got some back all right, but with little damage done.

On March 1st we relieved No. 4 Company in the front line; a minor raid was in contemplation, but owing to the brightness of the moon it had so far not been found practicable to carry it out.

Our trenches faced St. Pierre Vaast Wood, the Germans being just on the west fringe of it. It was a pretty peaceful place; the German infantry were quite inactive, and allowed us to show ourselves as much as we liked. The line was held by a series of posts holding from six to twelve men each; the posts were pretty close to the Germans, and one German shouted across that he was a barber in Bermondsey before the war, and he wished to God he was still!

The German here was quite a gentleman, but we apparently took too much advantage of his gentleness to please him, and he put up a notice in his trench that he didn't mind us carrying out reliefs in full view, but if we continued working parties he would be obliged to fire. This type of German was very rare, and it was really rather a danger, as one never knew when a relief might take place and the old Prussian type take his place.

The overdue raid took place on the night of the 3rd, under Lieutenant K. Henderson, with men from No. 2 Company; they reached the objective all right, but found the German was no longer occupying it, so the victory was barren.

At dawn on the 4th, our neighbours on our right did a show at Bouchavesnes, and our artillery did the same as on the previous occasion; we also prepared to let off smoke bombs, but the wind changed and that part of the show was off.

We had two naval officers attached to us at this time; one of them stayed to watch this little show, the other expressed a desire to see how the shells were brought up to the heavy guns in the rear. I think the one who stayed was duly impressed with the modern land battle; they were good fellows, but they took up rather a lot of room in our somewhat conscribed dugout.

The Germans replied fairly heartily, and some of our posts had rather a warm time.

We returned to Maurepas that night, on relief by the Scots Guards.

Two days later I left for England for my month's leave.

A prisoner recently captured had given away the secret that they were going to start withdrawing to the Hindenburg line on March 15th; the authorities believed this, but we, I think, were a bit sceptical. It turned out to be quite correct, as will be shown in the next chapter.

Chapter 16

The German Retirement and After

I was on leave till April 10th. During the time I was away things had been happening; the Germans had cleared off according to programme; they had two very good reasons for doing so: (1) to take up a new and properly defended trench system; owing to our continued pressure since the summer, they had had no opportunity to dig themselves properly in; (2) to upset our plans for a big attack along the whole front. Both these objects they achieved, but at a cost of much loss of morale on their side, and much gain of morale on ours.

So on the whole I think we may claim the operation as a success for us; it was the sequel of all the hard fighting of 1916; whatever view those in authority took of it, it was particularly pleasing to us in the fighting line, it being the first real movement since 1914. The actual ground gained was valueless, the Germans having destroyed everything ruthlessly, a policy which they pursued in all subsequent retirements, always given that they had the time. Many booby traps were left behind, and there was full scope for his artful cunning and dirty tricks.

I missed all this part. I wrote to the commanding officer asking if I should curtail my leave, as I thought we might be having casualties, but his very definite reply of "Whoever heard of a Grenadier returning to duty before the end of his leave?" put my mind at rest!

The battalion had advanced through St. Pierre Vaast Wood up to the village of Manancourt, after which troops of other divisions who had been resting took up the pursuit.

Thus, I found them at the same spot as I had left them, at Maurepas. They had had substantially no change in the battalion.

Our next job was of a less heroic nature, but most useful and important—that of making roads and railways in the conquered territory.

At first we worked on the road just east of Combles; we did this up to the 16th; it was monotonous work rather, but the men worked like niggers, and received nothing but praise from the staff.

On the 16th we moved back to Clery-sur-Somme, near Peronne, for a week's intensive training; we were under canvas, and we made the most of our week, and got through an immense amount of work.

On the 26th we went fatiguing again, this time on a railway. We camped at Le Mesnil, and were engaged laying a track up to Ytres and Fins, which were to be the new forward railheads. We used to rise at crack of dawn and work most of the day.

This went on till May 12th. We had rather fun at Le Mesnil. I got away to Amiens for one week-end; we used to stay at the Hotel du Rhin, and eat enormous meals at the Godbert or Cathedral restaurants.

On May 12th I was transferred to No. 1 Company as second in command to Craigie; Frank Eaton gave up the adjutancy and took command of No. 2, with Hirst under him; Mildmay came out from England as adjutant. The other officers in No. 1 were Frank Siltzer, Elliott and Fitzgerald.

The war had been very quiet on this front; the enemy seemed to have no aeroplanes, and we never got bombed or shelled.

On the 12th we returned to Clery, our first step in the direction of the Ypres Salient, to which we were destined to return.

On the 16th the King of the Belgians reviewed the 2nd Guards' Brigade (3rd Batt. Grenadiers, 1st Batt. Coldstream, 1st Batt. Scots Guards, 2nd Batt. Irish Guards), and a very good show it was. The men turned out remarkably well, and it was a marvel how smart they were in every way after a winter in the mud and a spring of doing Labour Corps work. No. 1 Company were a particularly fine lot of men just then, and I always remember the four men selected for commanding officer's escort on that day, three of them six feet five, and the fourth six feet three.

On the 17th we were on the move again; one night at Billon Farm, and then back to Ville-sur-Ancre, next door to Morlancourt, whence we had started for the Somme battlefield in the previous September. Here we stayed for a fortnight, resting and training, and it was one of the pleasantest times we had during the war.

We were all very happy at being rid of the Somme mud and all its horrible associations; the billets were good, and Amiens wasn't far off, and altogether we were full of the "*joie de vivre.*"

The country round here was charming; especially I remember a little place called Heilly, which boasted a restaurant and tea shop; I fear it was destroyed in 1918 in the German advance.

On the 30th three companies went on with their journey, and we were left to clean up, and followed next day; our destination was Wardrecques, near St. Omer. It was a camp, and here, too, we were well off.

Here we stayed till June 12th, in reserve for the Messines battle, and incidentally training for our own offensive which was to come. We also put in some musketry on the ranges at Moringhem, staying two nights there.

The annual Fourth of June Eton dinner took place at St. Omer; this year it was open to the whole of the 14th Corps, and there were over two hundred people present.

On the 12th we set off for the war once more, stopping at Wormhout and Watou *en route* for Elverdinghe.

Colonel Thorne left us at Wardrecques on sick leave, and Major Rasch took command.

CHAPTER 17

Ypres Salient, 1917

Our next job was to take over the extreme left of the British line, next to the Belgians: Our line there was very short, and was held with only one battalion in the front lines; the remainder of the division was distributed in depth; one brigade right back at Herzeele, one in the forest area, and one in front.

It took our brigade to go up first, but not our battalion, so we had a bit of time first at Elverdinghe and neighbourhood, and later at a farm further forward.

For the first few days my company lived in cellars in the village; our cellar was just at a cross road, and most unhealthy, it being a favourite spot to be shelled.

I was commanding the company temporarily, as John Craigie was acting second in command. When the battalion went forward to the Bleuet Farm area, east of Elverdinghe, in support, Craigie returned to the company, Ridley having come from England as second in command, and I was sent back to the transport lines for a few days. These were not far from Poperinghe, where we used to go most days. There were pierrot shows there, and cinemas, and a new restaurant called "Cyril's," which we used to patronise.

On the 22nd I returned to the company, which had returned to the Elverdinghe area, and were in dugouts along the kitchen garden wall of the *château*; it sounds a peaceful sort of place, but was in reality anything but. There was a battery of our 8-inch howitzers in some trees just beyond the garden, and the Germans discovered these and shelled them unmercifully all day on the 24th; it was not too pleasant for us, as the shells just cleared our wall, and the short ones just didn't. So in the evening we moved to huts just behind, known as Roussol Farm; the rest of the battalion were already there.

On the 26th we relieved the 1st Battalion Scots Guards in the front line.

The line ran just west of the Yser Canal, in front of Boesinghe, and the Germans were just the other side of the canal, so we were very close; the canal was pretty low, and with the aid of mats it was possible to cross in places.

The trenches were pretty good, and the actual front line had been quiet up to then. The village of Boesinghe, where battalion headquarters were and the reserve company, was always getting shelled, and was one of the unhealthiest spots on the Western front. We didn't get shelled much, but had a lot of trouble from trench mortar bombs at night. These were known as pineapples, and exploded with a terrific noise; they used to blow out our candles in our dugout, and were generally disconcerting. We had bad luck from one on the 28th, in the early morning; a pineapple dropped right among our company H.Q. staff, and killed my servant, Hucklesby, who was lying asleep, set off a box of Verey lights, and severely wounded two or three other men, including John Craigie's servant, who lost a leg.

Apart from this incident, things were pretty quiet, except for showers of rifle grenades during our relief by the 3rd Batt. Coldstream on the evening of the 28th.

After relief we marched back to a camp in the Forest at a place called Coppernollehoek, a typical name for this part of the world. There we were in tents; we only had two nights there, but one of them was most disturbed by the German long range guns starting a sudden and furious bombardment of our camp in the middle of the night. It was a wonderful scene—officers in pyjamas running about everywhere trying to get their men out of their bivouacs into the emergency trenches dug for such an occasion as this. Not much damage was done, except to a man on sentry; the battalion sergeant-major's tent was missed by a fraction.

It is not nice being shelled in the dark, with nothing but a piece of canvas over one's head, but we got a good deal of it in the summer of 1917, and later got inured to it.

On July 1st the 2nd Brigade went back to Herzeele, where an exact imitation of the German positions to be attacked in the coming offensive was laid out. And every day we practised this attack over the canal and over the Pilkem ridge.

I was detailed to command the company in the fight, having with me Siltzer and Elliot, Craigie and Fitzgerald being left out. We got pretty well word perfect by the time we left; sand models in minute detail were laid out, and we spent hours studying them with our N.C.O.'s.

Herzeele was a nice place, well away from the war, and we billeted in farm houses.

H.M. the King came and watched us doing a practice one day.

We had one officer casualty here, Allan Adair falling off a bicycle and putting out his shoulder; as I lent him the bike, an old French one with many weaknesses, I felt in some measure responsible!

We returned to the east end of the forest on the 13th. Colonel Thorne had meanwhile re-joined, and although missing the training, very soon knew more about the coming offensive than any of us. Next day we moved further forward to a bivouac near De Wippe Cabaret, west of Elverdinghe. This place was surrounded with our guns massing for the attack.

From here we did continual fatigues to the front line, getting the attack ready. Meanwhile, the Germans got wind of something about to happen, and their shelling increased. Fatigues at night were perilous affairs. They generally centred round Boesinghe, which in ordinary times was no bed of roses, but now became an inferno. I remember one particularly dreadful night when I took up ninety men to carry heavy 290 lbs. trench mortar bombs from a store in Boesinghe up to the gun position. It was a dreadful night, pitch dark, with shells pouring down; we worked as well as we could, but the difficulties were immense. On the way home down the communication trenches we were shelled all the way, shells just skimming over the sides of them; I have a very vivid recollection of that night.

On the 18th I had the interesting experience of being shelled in the dentist's chair. This, was at the C.C.S. near St. Sixte, which was a favourite target for the German naval gunners.

We had some close shaves, too, in our bivouac from the quick-firing naval guns, but got off with nothing worse than occasional showers of earth.

Meanwhile, plans for the attack were proceeding apace; the actual date was still unknown.

The battalion had to do one more tour of duty in the line before the great day. They went up on the 21st; as far as possible those taking part in the battle were left behind, including myself. The battalion had a bad time this tour, chiefly from gas; the Germans now were expecting the attack any morning, and used to barrage the whole of our forward area with gas every dawn.

Our preparatory bombardment, to last ten days or so, had now started, and the face of the country the other side of the canal was being gradually changed and blackened out of recognition. The Germans there must have had a dreadful time.

The battalion was relieved on the 28th, much exhausted from continual use of gas helmets; we lost several good men in the company from shell fire, too; and altogether they must have had a very unpleasant time.

Next day there were signs of a German withdrawal. They had apparently cleared off from their forward positions, being unable to stand our fire any more, and there seemed a possibility of our attack plans being upset. But it was decided to cross the canal before zero day, occupy the old German line, and carry on the old plan, only starting a few hundred yards to the good. This crossing the canal was carried out by the 3rd Batt. Coldstream, who were to be in reserve on the day; they did the job most brilliantly, and it was a great advantage to us having the crossings made good.

On the 27th we had a battalion dinner in our bivouac; a truly wonderful repast was produced, chiefly from Poperinghe, and all went very merrily till a German aeroplane came over and dropped bombs on us and causing us to put out the lights.

Next day, the 28th, we were told it was W. day, denoting the 31st as Z. day.

Chapter 18

The Pilkem Offensive

And so we got to the eve of the great offensive.

The offensive was unlike its predecessors of the Somme and Loos from our point of view, and in two respects—firstly, we had to do all the preparatory work and then the attack itself; secondly, we were to take part in the opening day, instead of being kept to be pushed through the gap if created. The latter was an advantage undoubtedly, but the former involved a tremendous amount of work, and of a most dangerous nature. Thus it was that many men never lived to fight in the great battle they had rehearsed so minutely, and which they had prepared for so carefully. There was one man who was to be the right-hand man of our line, and he was particularly proud of being "the right-hand man of the Guards' Division," as he called it, but he never lived to fulfil that role, being killed by a shell a week before.

All the battalions in the division suffered in this preliminary work; we were perhaps luckier than most in that we had no officers hit; our 2nd Battalion was unlucky in this respect, losing two valuable officers on patrol, in Basil Blackwood and Gunnis; they patrolled across the canal, and neither of them were seen again.

And speaking of this incident makes me think of the fine part played by the "old" men of the regiment in the war; I am thinking of the men well over forty who joined up in a fighting regiment as ensigns, serving readily and cheerfully under men half their own age. Basil Blackwood was a special example of this, and others I could mention are Alfred Yorke, Frank Siltzer, Aubrey Hall, Gerald Arbuthnot; there were others also, and the other regiments of the brigade had similar instances. These men, not far short of fifty years old, indeed put to shame those myriads, much younger, who stayed at home or found soft jobs behind the line.

The 1st Batt. Coldstream had very bad luck in losing their commanding officer and second in command (Colonel Hopwood and Major Burton), killed by the same shell on their way back from inspecting the front line. There was a cemetery just behind known as Canada Farm; in the middle of June it was practically empty; by July 31st it was nearly full, all Guardsmen killed preparing for the great battle.

On the 30th we were to go up to the assembly positions preparatory to attacking at dawn next morning. These assembly positions had been heavily shelled with gas shells every morning for the past ten days between 3 and 4.30 a.m., and as there seemed no reason for the Germans to alter their habits, we fully expected to have an awkward time before getting off the mark.

We spent the 30th putting the finishing touches to the arrangements, in a state of pent-up excitement, trying to appear calm, but inwardly seething.

The plan of attack, put very briefly, was this—the 2nd and 3rd Guards' Brigades were to start off the attack, the 2nd on the right. Two battalions of each brigade were to capture the first and second objectives; the other two battalions were to pass through to the third; finally, two battalions of the 1st Guards' Brigade were to go through to the fourth objective over the stream known as the Steenbeck.

We will only concern ourselves with the doings of the 2nd Guards' Brigade on the right.

The 1st Batt. Scots Guards and the 2nd Batt. Irish Guards were to take the first and second objectives; the 1st Batt. Coldstream were to pass through the Irish Guards, and we were to pass through the Scots Guards, and eventually the 2nd Batt. Grenadiers were to pass through the whole brigade. My company (I was in command, Craigie being left out) was to be on the right with No. 2, under Frank Eaton, on my left, and with No. 3, under Neville, in close support, and No. 4, under Heasman, in reserve.

So much for the plans; and now for the execution thereof.

We left our camp soon after dark on the 30th, and halted just east of Elverdinghe, where we drank rum and tea, which was most comforting, especially the former beverage! and then on by platoons to the assembly positions, just south-west of Boesinghe village.

One of my platoons was lost in the dark, and gave me many anxious moments; it luckily turned up five minutes before zero hour.

The battle was to start at 3.50 a.m., but we weren't due to move till 5 o'clock.

That night and morning will ever remain a mystery to me; I mentioned just now that the particular spot we were to assemble in was shelled to bits every morning. Well, on this night 30th-31st not a shell of any sort or size came anywhere near us; our guns were firing hard all night, but not a word came from the other side; it was a merciful thing, and saved us an incalculable amount of trouble. There were two official views of this: (1) most favoured by gunners, that our counter battery fire was so good that not a German could get near his guns to fire them'; (2) that the German gunners were busy getting their guns away and over the Steenbeck river to avoid our capturing them.

At 3.50 precisely Hell was let loose, as the war correspondents would say; Hell had been let loose many times before, but I doubt if she got quite so much off the chain as on this memorable morning. The barrage was terrific, and a battery of machine guns doing overhead fire just behind us added to the din.

At 5 a.m. we got on the move, on through the slimy mud in artillery formation or "platoon blobs"; my officers under me were Siltzer and Elliott. We crossed the canal on improvised bridges made of petrol tins; it was ticklish work; a false step would have pitched one into a filthy morass which was known as the Yser Canal.

As I said in a previous chapter, we had studied the ground to be advanced over from every point of view, and knew just how many roads we had to cross and the position of every tree. But when we got across the canal, we found all landmarks gone—roads obliterated, woods only shadows of their former selves; and it was no easy job to find the various objectives. We were to go up to the second objective, and form up behind the Scots Guards, and advance again when the barrage re-started.

Well, everything seemed to be going according to plan, and we were having one of the halts as laid down in the programme; we saw men, presumably Scots Guards, advancing away in front of us, when the commanding officer (Colonel Thorne) came up to me and told me we were already the foremost troops, that the men we saw in front were Germans retiring, and that the Scots Guards, owing to heavy casualties, had not been able to get beyond the first objective, consequently we were to go on and make good the second objective, and then go on to our own.

On arrival at the second objective, a company of Scots Guards, under Captain Bradshaw, arrived and took over the line, and we continued the advance. All this time we were much bothered by enemy machine guns fired from concrete blockhouses, known after as "pill boxes," all along the Ypres-Staden railway, which was our right, and the boundary between us and the 38th Welsh Division. The Welsh Division were going well, but were a trifle behind, so we had to deal with these pill-boxes; and their occupants surrendered as soon as we got quite close, and came running out without equipment and crying for mercy; we spared them, but no one could have blamed us if we had butchered the lot, they having fired at us as long as we were a safe distance away, and then expecting mercy. One of them offered me a drink of his coffee as a peace offering; I declined the kind offer, and showed him the road to captivity.

No. 3 Company, behind us, were of the greatest assistance to us, and came up and reinforced our right.

We eventually reached our objective, which had been a road, but was now only just recognisable as such; and we started to dig in.

During the advance we had very little hostile shell fire, but when we arrived at our final objective, their guns started, and once started they never stopped; they were luckily inaccurate, and we were able to get quite respectable cover. Meanwhile No. 2 Company had done well, and had reached their allotted position on our left, having a good haul of prisoners from a ruined house *en route.*

A diversion was caused during the advance by an old hare getting up and running down the line; several people blazed at it, but when last seen it was running strongly, and disappeared into the Welsh lines.

We had now reached the edge of the absolutely devastated area, and there was grass growing in front of us and a few respectable trees; so when the 2nd Batt. went through us they had rather a stiff proposition; there was much machine gun and rifle fire.

I can imagine many battalions being held up in a similar position, but it was a tradition of the brigade that the allotted objective must be reached, up to the very last yard of ground, so the 2nd Batt. went on and made good the line of the Steenbeck; it was not too pleasant for them; the division on the right were a bit held up, and it was some time before they came up in line.

Away on our left the 3rd Brigade had accomplished their task, and the 2nd Battalion Coldstream had gone through them; further on the left the French had been brilliant, and the day had been a great success. The actual ground gained was valueless, being a mere morass, but we had captured many prisoners and lowered the enemy's morale; moreover, we had straightened out the north end of the Salient and had captured Pilkem ridge; thus the Ypres Salient was no longer; that ancient terror was removed. Whether our eventual retirement in 1918 re-made the Salient I don't quite know, but at any rate it had gone for the moment.

So much for the achievement, but what had it cost us?

For a first class offensive we reckoned we had got off lightly; my company lost about fifty *per cent.*, and one officer (Elliott) wounded; we went in 117 and marched out 48 strong; a few more turned up later, being mixed up with other companies; our percentage of killed was luckily small. The battalion had one officer killed, Bryan Dunlop; he was a great loss, being a very promising officer, and popular with everybody.

Well, the attack being over, we set to work to consolidate the new position.

As we were no longer front line troops, my company was brought back to battalion H.Q., where we dug new trenches that night, incidentally getting a few hours' sleep; I was lucky to find a place to lie down in, a captured pill-box, and had a really good sleep.

It had meanwhile started raining, and it poured all night and next day. This was very hard on the men after all they had already gone through. We had a bit of bad luck that night in a stray shell getting a direct hit on one of our new trenches and killing three men.

Frank Siltzer, my only remaining officer, did fine work all this time, and was a wonderful example of coolness. I have often regretted that I didn't recommend him for a decoration.

Next day was a day of rain and shells, but of no particular interest otherwise; we were all wet and exhausted, but happy at our success and looking forward to a wash and sleep on being relieved. The 1st Battalion Irish Guards relieved us in the evening.

It was a hard journey back through the mud, which had become infinitely worse; but once on to decent roads again, beyond Boesinghe everyone cheered up, and we started a song, and the remains of the company marched back to the forest victoriously, singing as they went. It was a proud moment, and the feeling of satisfaction increased on arriving in camp and finding a champagne supper laid out ready for us.

That night we slept the sleep of the just.

CHAPTER 19

The Pilkem Offensive (Continued)

We only had two nights' rest, returning to the line on August 3rd.

We weren't in the actual front line this time, but took over the area captured by the 2nd Guards' Brigade on the 31st; the 1st Battalion Scots Guards took over the Steenbeck line. But although only in support, we had a warmish time from shells, and it rained almost continuously.

I had my H.Q. in a pill-box in Abri Wood, and the Germans enjoyed having pot shots at it all day.

We didn't have too pleasant a walk on the first night, and the Germans started a heavy barrage just as we got up, and this delayed the relief a good deal, and it was some time before we got finally settled in.

We lost an officer, Webster, killed that night; the son of an old grenadier, he was particularly popular with everyone, and would have been a fine soldier had he lived.

There is not much more to say about these two days; it was very wet and miserable, and it was courting death to walk about; the German was thoroughly roused by now, and shelled like anything, fearing we should continue our advance.

On the 5th we were relieved by King's Company of our 1st Battalion, under Leo Fisher-Rowe. It was what might be called a very "windy" night, and many shells were flying about, and I remember doing excellent time over the duckboards with my C.S.M. and orderly after the relief was complete.

That night we went back to Herzeele by lorry, and two days later I went on Paris leave with Frank Eaton; Paris didn't seem at all a bad place after Pilkem and Boesinghe, and we didn't do ourselves too badly there. But as this is supposed to be a story of the war, I will not write anything about Paris life.

We returned on the 12th.

On the 14th the battalion left for de Wippe Cabaret camp in reserve for an attack by the 29th (?) Division; I was left behind with the details at Herzeele, and Craigie took the company up. As a matter of fact they had no fighting to do, only a few fatigues, and returned intact on the 19th.

At this time our brigadier (Brigadier-General John Ponsonby) left to command a division. I doubt if any commander was ever more popular with his troops, and his departure was very much felt. He was succeeded by Brigadier-General Brooke, who had commanded the battalion on the Somme, an appointment which gave the greatest satisfaction to all of us; he remained in command, except for a short absence, gassed, till the brigade returned from Germany.

We amused ourselves well enough at Herzeele, and had cricket matches, and on the 25th our Transport Officer, Duquenoy, produced a wonderful and most realistic Wild West Show, and we entertained all the women and children of Herzeele, who seemed much impressed.

Next day I went on leave, returning on September 5th.

I found the battalion had gone forward again, and was doing fatigues from a camp called Eton Camp, near Woesten and Elverdinghe. The night before I rejoined they had had a catastrophe; No. 1 Company had been on fatigue in front, and had just got back to camp, and were having some hot drinks, when a German aeroplane came over and dropped bombs and laid out thirty of them. Naval guns used to fire on the camp too, at intervals, so it wasn't too salubrious a spot.

There was another small offensive operation in view, a sort of glorified raid really; it was to be a one-company show really, and No. 4, under Hirst, was to do the dirty work. There was much preparation, and practices over a reproduction made nearby of the country to be attacked; later, the scheme became more ambitious, and was to involve the whole battalion. It was to take place on the 15th, the anniversary of that terrible day on the Somme. In the end the idea was dropped, probably as likely to be more costly than the objects warranted.

I got in for an unpleasant fatigue, pushing trolleys on a Decauville line up to the front battalion H.Q.; the trucks were heavily laden with corrugated iron, and every few yards of course came off the line. There was the usual accompanying bombardment going on, of course; and at one time things looked awkward, and we had to lie very close to the mud to escape a tornado of 4.2 shells which centred round our miserable truck, which we were then trying to persuade to get on the line again. It was a typical "battle fatigue," with mud, shells and darkness all contributing to its unpleasantness.

On the 13th we moved a bit further to Rugby Camp, which was on the same lines as Eton Camp, but with all its disadvantages accentuated.

The day before leaving for this resort, a flight of aeroplanes came over the camp at lunch time, and dropped a shower of bombs on us, luckily doing little damage. They hit an officer of No. 3 Company, Borthwick, who was sitting peacefully lunching; our company was having a lunch party, and were busy eating *foie gras*; some of us retired to a safer place, others remained eating *foie gras*, too engrossed to take notice!

We took over Rugby Camp from our 2nd Battalion; they had been heavily gas shelled there, and did not report well on the place.

There were two 1.2-inch howitzers just behind, not fifty yards from our mess, and the noise they made firing shook the whole of one's inside up. As a rule they fired for two hours every afternoon. It was awful for us; at night the Germans used to search for them with 9-inch shells, which used to fizz over the top of our tents; sleeping was a matter of some difficulty there.

One evening there we practised a night patrol, but the practice became too realistic, owing to the German shells, so it was deemed wiser to abandon it!

On Sunday, the 16th, we had a church parade among all the din; it was taken by the senior chaplain of the division, the Rev. F. W. Head, who had been our battalion chaplain previously. He was a remarkable man, and the men absolutely worshipped him; wherever the battle was hottest there he was to be found talking to the men, as oblivious to danger as though in his own parish at home. I remember him preaching that night, and saying what a wonderful month September had always been for the British army during the war; and if one comes to think of it, no month of the year was fuller of incident—the Aisne in 1914, Loos in 1915, the Somme in 1916, the Bronbeck in 1917, and later, in 1918, the Canal du Nord and the breaking of the Hindenburg Line.

On the 17th we relieved the 1st Battalion Scots Guards on the Bronbeck, in front of Langemarck. There had been trouble a day or two before, the Germans attempting to rush our forward posts; the 2nd Battalion Irish Guards were involved, and as a result of the fight two of their men got V.C.'s.

Once again we had an unpleasant walk up. My company was to be in the front line, with No. 2 on our left; a torrent of shells greeted our arrival. We had our company H.Q. in a post a little bit back from the front ones; the company was spread about in posts in front; the Bronbeck stream ran between us and the enemy.

On the 20th there was to be a big attack on our right; the troops immediately south of us were to take part, and although we weren't to move, there was to be an intense barrage on our part of the line.

Tuesday, the 18th, was a day of smart shelling by both sides, and one didn't feel too happy. On the 19th an intercepted German message foretold an attack on our front at dawn, and I was sent up into one of the front posts in case anything happened; we put down a barrage, partly as a protection in case of enemy attack, and partly as a practice for the 20th. I stayed in a rickety pill-box there, and got nearly all the men under cover too, except for sentries. The Germans shelled hard too for an hour or so, and the noise of shells bursting caused an awful vibration inside the pill-box, and one felt one would go mad if it lasted much longer. There was no German attack, however, but it was a noisy day; we did another practice barrage later in the day, which caused the usual response.

Next morning at 5.40 a.m. the big attack on our right started; the idea, I think, was to straighten the line a bit, as we on the left of the British line were a bit ahead of the rest, and they were to endeavour to get into line preparatory to a further general advance.

We were to withdraw from our forward posts to allow the barrage to come down on the Bronbeck line; this we did, advancing again behind the barrage to our old positions.

The rest of that day was much like its predecessors, continuous shelling, making these four days in the Bronbeck sector memorable as one of our most shelly experiences.

Next day, the 21st, a battalion of the Essex regiment came to relieve us. The Germans put down another barrage just before the relief arrived.

I was ordered to take one of our platoons out after relief, and I nearly led them to disaster, getting completely lost. It happened thus:

We had sent a guide to bring in the Essex regiment, and as I was a bit doubtful of the way back in the dark, I told this man to lead us out; well, he started off, fell down twice in shell holes in the first twenty yards, and after leading us round in circles a few times had to admit he had no idea where we were; so I took up the leading, which indeed I should have done to begin with. I thought I had hit off the right direction; my aim was to march on the sound of our guns firing, hoping to run into someone who would put us in the right way. I thought I could distinguish between the noise British guns made firing and the noise German guns made firing; but I was wrong, I couldn't! Thus, after floundering along for some time in the pitch dark and through the mud, we had begun to think we must be a mile or two from the line, when suddenly a Verey light shot up and fell over our heads, thus indicating that we were only about thirty yards from the Germans. I have never been so taken aback in my life. Here were we, some twenty-five or thirty men, in full kit, all carrying petrol cans, clanking along, with a certain amount of talking going on, walking straight into the German lines. We had evidently got through our own lines between the posts, and were now in No Man's Land!

Well, this required a little thought; so we all lay down, while I sought for a solution. Luckily I thought of studying the heavens, and without being an astronomer in any way, I happened to know the North star when I saw it. Well, we were at that moment heading straight for the North star, when we should be going due south to get to our rest billets. So the solution seemed simple—just turn about and walk straight; so we did this, leaving our petrol cans for fear of making too much noise. Though I didn't realise it at the time, not having recovered from the shock, our troubles were not over, as we had to get through to our lines again, and one couldn't be certain of striking a gap again; so before we had gone far we were sharply challenged in English by the voice of a sergeant I knew well, "Halt, who are you?"

"Grenadiers, of course; who do you think?" answered I innocently.

They, of course, thought we were Germans; the whole platoon post was standing to arms with bayonets sticking over the top of the parapet ready for us, and there was a machine gunner with his finger on the trigger just waiting for the word to fire! It was a lucky escape, and it speaks well for our fire control that no one let his rifle off before the challenging; also why the Germans were content with one Verey light only, and didn't fire at us, I have never made out. It was a bad business, my fault of course, but I felt very angry with the guide for disappointing my faith in him, and on arrival in camp I put him in arrest, but next morning he was released, it having been borne in upon me that it was my fault and no one else's.

That night we entrained for Proven, where we were in camp till the 29th, when we moved back to Herzeele to practice for the next attack. This training went on till October 5th; it was a good rest, too, and the battalion was refreshed for further efforts.

I was to be left out of the next attack, so when the battalion went off, I remained behind with the details.

Next day I left for England on special leave, and while on leave I got orders that my "six months' home duty," which I had been recommended for, had come through; so the war saw me no more till May, 1918. I had had over three years' continuous service in France, so that I was glad to get home for a bit, though I was feeling particularly fit at that time, and morale was very high. Hirst also came back for six months; it was a War Office scheme, and continued till the end of the war.

CHAPTER 20

Six Months at Home

I do not propose to deal at any length with these six months.

I did duty at Chelsea Barracks with the 5th Reserve Battalion under Lord Francis Scott. Our only excitement was from air raids, which were particularly numerous at this time; they entailed a certain number of officers returning to barracks at once and waiting till the "All clear" was sounded; I only got caught once this way, so was lucky.

There was one air raid which affected us more than others, in that it caused the death of an old and much respected grenadier, Captain Ludlow, who had just taken over a post at Chelsea Hospital; he had been regimental sergeant-major of the 2nd Battalion when I first joined, and later quartermaster of the 4th Battalion; in the end he was invalided home and given this job. It was a particularly distressing affair, as his wife and several children were killed too, and his loss was very much felt.

Although life was pleasant at home, many big things were happening out in France. I am not going to describe the battles which took place during that time, as I was not there myself, but I will just give a brief outline of what had occurred during my time at home.

On October 9th the Guards' Division attacked from the Bronbeck position, and on that day and a subsequent one advanced up to the outskirts of Houthoulst Forest; it was a well organised show, and the casualties were comparatively light; the battalion lost three officers killed, Tetley, Greenhill and Roper; the former was commanding No. 3 Company at the time, and was a man of peculiar charm and ability. They were all three great losses to the battalion.

After a rest, the division was moved south to take part in the new Cambrai battle, and at the end of November the battalion fought a most heroic battle at Fontaine Notre Dame, near Bourlon Wood; they captured the village after a desperate struggle, and after suffering very heavily, but in the end had to fight their way put, the Germans having got round behind them; thus this great effort was wasted owing to lack of support on the flanks.

This attack was carried out by the 2nd Guards' Brigade.

The battalion lost many fine men that day; among the officers, Beaumont, Nesbit, Worsley and Bowes-Lyon, all of whom had served the regiment well over a long period, were killed, and there were others wounded.

A day or two later the division did its famous counter-attack at Gouzaucourt, and saved the army from a very ugly disaster. This was carried out by the 1st and 3rd Guards' Brigades, and was one of the finest achievements of the whole war.

Following this, the division moved to Arras, and took over trenches in the Roeux-Fampoux area; here the remainder of the winter was spent fairly quietly.

In March the imminence of a big German offensive became certain, and the greatest vigilance was required from all front-line troops; as it turned out, the division was relieved the day before the storm broke (March 21st), and were billeted in Arras. When the attack developed, they were moved south to the Ervillers district, where the attack had made some progress; they restored the situation there, and held their line intact against all assaults. The line in this part, when the offensive was brought to a stop, ran just west of Hamelincourt, Moyenville and Courcelles le Conte, and east of Boiry St. Martin and Ayette, and they were still holding this line when I rejoined in May.

During this latter fighting the battalion had lost several officers—Ralph Parker, Orriss, Pauling, Durbin and Van Ranney killed, and several wounded; the former had been a particular friend of mine, and was commanding No. 1 Company when he was hit by a machine gun bullet.

CHAPTER 21

Boiry St. Martin

On May 1st my six months was up, and I went on leave till I was required to go back to France.

I eventually left London on the night of May 13th-14th, and on arrival in France was sent to the Base Camp at Etaples; Hirst returned with me. Etaples was not our own base, and after a few days there we were moved on to Havre to our own depôt.

On the way there we passed through Abbeville while an air raid was in progress, and I have never known a French train move so quickly; it simply crashed through that town, and it was some time before it resumed its normal lethargic methods.

Havre was much as it always was, a comfortable camp, good food, and general air of well-being; the weather was very hot, and we bathed most days.

On the 24th we got our orders for the front, and we left that night, spending the next day at Rouen, finally detraining at War-lincourt near Saulty, thence proceeding to St. Amand, where the battalion's details were.

The battalion had undergone many changes; Colonel Thorne still commanded, Lord Lascelles was second in command; company commanders as follows: (1) Wiggins, (2) Drury, (3) Tufnell, (4) Bedford.

On the 27th I left St. Amand to join the battalion at a place called "Rabbit Wood," just west of Adinfer; they were due to go into the trenches that evening.

On arrival at Rabbit Wood I was greeted by the commanding officer by the information that I had arrived just in time, as the Germans were going to attack at 3 a.m. next morning!

I was put to command No. 3 Company, in the temporary absence of Tufnell. Hirst got No. 4 Company again. The other officers in No. 3 were Godman, Clifton Brown, Duff Cooper and Gibbon; the two latter accompanied me into the trenches that night.

We got shelled going up near Adinfer, and I found I soon got used to the experience again, and I found it no more pleasant than before. Our trenches were just south-east of Boiry St. Martin; the front line was held in various posts, with the C.H.Q. under a bank. It was fairly peaceful there except for dawn and dusk each day, when the Germans barraged us. They did not attack us next day; on the other hand, it seemed more as if they rather expected us to.

On the 30th, No. 1 Company relieved us, and we went back to a bank near Valley Wood; there were dugouts, and not too bad. We had two quiet days there, and the war didn't seem to be such a dangerous occupation as it was when I left it.

On the early morning of the 2nd, about 2 a.m., the Germans started gas shelling the whole forward area; it was still dark, so it was no very easy job waking everyone up and getting their gas helmets on; I think therefore it reflects great credit on the company, and speaks well for their training and discipline, that we didn't have a single casualty from gas, although the shelling was heavy, lasting over an hour, and there was no wind at all to blow the gas away. I wore my gas helmet for an hour continuously, and can't say I enjoyed it much,

Next day we returned to Rabbit Wood, and Tufnell rejoined the company next day, I remaining as his second in command.

On the 4th all Old Etonians went back to St. Amand for the usual dinner, returning next day to Rabbit Wood.

On the 7th the Division was relieved by the 2nd Division, the 2nd Battalion Oxford and Bucks L. I. taking over from us.

We marched back to a place called La Bazecque Farm, east of Saulty; here we were partly under canvas and partly in farm buildings. All being well, we were to have a clear month's training here.

The Germans seemed to have given up their attacks against the British, and were putting all their force against the French. further south.

We put in a tremendous amount of training and recreation at La Bazecque, and at. the end of our month were fit for anything. A curious epidemic, known as "Spanish 'flu," or P.U.O., spread over the battalion, and nearly everyone got it; it lasted from two to seven days, so was not really serious, but it made one feel very ill.

We had brigade and battalion sports and a divisional race meeting and a horse show and a certain amount of cricket. We were occasionally reminded of the war by hostile aircraft dropping bombs or by long range guns firing at us; on the 28th we had a practice alarm, and we marched up to our battle positions near Pommier; we didn't know till we got there that it was only practice, and we went up prepared to beat back the enemy. It was a very hot day., and I was just starting P.U.O., so I was glad we had nothing more serious to do.

On the 6th July the battalion left for the front line again; I went with the details to Bailleulmont, and Tufnell took the company in.

Bailleulmont was quite a nice village, and practically unharmed. The details of the 1st and 2nd Guards' Brigades were quartered there. I stayed there till the 17th, when I returned to the battalion at Ransart, where they were in reserve in bivouac and trenches.

On the 18th we took over the front system again, just north of where I had been before, and due east of Boiry St. Martin, in which place B.H.Q. were. The front line was held by one company, with two others in the Boiry sunken road in dugouts, and the 4th in and about the sugar factory further back.

It took us for the sugar factory first; it was a favourite target for the Germans, and had a very evil reputation before we finally left it.

After two days there we went into the front line, a line of posts of considerable length. Trench mortar bombs were the trouble here, and the slightest movement by day produced a hail of these.

After two days of these, we went back to the sunken road, which was the best position of the lot. The dugouts were good, and for some unknown reason it was never shelled. It was always swarming with life, and was altogether rather an interesting place; a famous artist came out from England and did a picture of it.

At this time we had some Americans attached for instruction; I had three of their officers attached; they kept us very busy answering questions, and seemed to have a wonderful grasp of the situation, considering they were new to it all.

When not in the front system, the battalion was either in support in trenches known as Hameau Switch and Windmill Switch, with B.H.Q. and the reserve company near Ransart, or in reserve at Ransart. When in reserve we were able to move about freely and do training and play games; but one had to be more careful in support, it being in the shelled area and among all our heavy guns.

On August 8th I was transferred to No. 1 Company to command it, Arthur Wiggins having gone to England as an instructor; .thus at last I got a company of my own, and I was particularly pleased at getting command of my old company; I had under me there Elliott, Clough Taylor, Delacombe, Calvocoressi and Carstairs, and later on Inglis Jones.

They were in Adinfer village at the time, and my first night with them was rather stormy, the Germans keeping up a continuous fire on the already ruined village. The battalion was back in the front lines again, and on the 10th carried out a raid against a supposed German strong point; de Geijer, the intelligence officer, was in charge of the operation, and the artillery put down a barrage; the raiding party reached its objective all right, but the Germans had cleared off, so no prisoners were taken.

On the 16th our usual routine was broken by a sudden order

to move back to Saulty. There was much conjecture as to what this meant, the official explanation given out being that the enemy were massing opposite us and a new attack was imminent, and therefore it had been decided that each division should have one complete brigade in reserve for counter attacking purposes, and that the 2nd Guards' Brigade had been selected to be in reserve for the Guards' Division. Well, everyone believed this at first, but personally I rather suspected something different, chiefly because we were told to practise counter attacking, and that if we did have to counter-attack we should be required to go past our original line and capture the village of Moyenneville, and therefore, as we already knew the features of the ground behind our own lines, special study must be made of that between our old line and Moyenneville.

Well, this looked to me much more like a plan for an offensive from our side, and so it proved to be; the previous story being circulated to prevent people talking and giving the show away.

At Saulty we prepared for the offensive, which was destined to be the beginning of the end, and which I will describe in the next chapter.

CHAPTER 22

The 1918 Offensive: (1) Moyenneville

The attack was due to start at crack of dawn on the 21st.

We had all learnt our parts as best we could; there had been many conferences and much poring over maps. We all knew our objectives on the map; those of us who had taken part in big offensives before were less sanguine of finding them easily on the actual ground.

Briefly, the plan of attack was this: The 2nd Guards' Brigade was to carry out the attack, the final objective of which was the Arras-Albert railway; the 1st Battalion Scots Guards were to start the attack on the right, with the 1st Battalion Coldstream on their left; we were to follow up the Scots Guards, and pass through them at their final objective, just as we had to at Pilkem in the previous year, and capture the line of the railway, some way on. The 2nd Battalion Irish Guards having been taken away from us, there was no one to pass through the Coldstream, so they had to do the full journey, though if I remember right they had a shorter front.

The preliminaries to this attack were much the same as those of previous attacks; in this case, though, there was more surprise attempted than before; there was none of that dreadful hammering we gave the Germans at Pilkem, and consequently it was easier for us taking up our positions.

Three officers per company only went into the attack; I had

Clough Taylor and Delacombe with me, though Carstairs, refusing to be left behind, joined us next day. Allan Adair took in No. 2 Company with Fairbairn and Chapman; Tufnell No. 3, with Clifton Brown and Duff Cooper; Hirst No. 4, with West and Papillon. As regards the battalion plans: Nos. 3 and 4 Companies were to be in front and capture the railway, No. 2 in support close behind, while my company, No. 1, was to be in reserve, and its objective was not far in advance of the Scots Guards. So it didn't seem as if we should have much of a show this time. When people told me I had got the "cushy" job this time, I remember thinking that we should most likely end up in front, this being so often the fate of intended reserves.

We left Saulty in motor lorries on the evening of the 20th, got out at the Hendecourt district and marched thence, after a halt for tea and rum, to our old friend the sunken road at Boiry St. Martin. Here we got the men as comfortable as possible, and told them to get some sleep if possible; the night was fine, but there was a mist coming on.

I remember getting a very good sleep that night; we had a hot breakfast somewhere between 3 and 4 a.m., having brought cooks and utensils up for the purpose, they afterwards returning to the transport. It was a funny sensation, waking out of a deep and untroubled sleep, and suddenly realising that one was about to pop the parapet, and more than this, that one was responsible for the handling of some 130 men, responsible for getting them to their objective with the least possible casualties.

By 4.30 a.m. we were all ready in our assembly positions, armed to the teeth, and ready for anything; the mist had developed into a fog, and one anticipated trouble in finding the way. At 4.55 the barrage started, and a very fine one it was; tanks were co-operating, and one didn't envy the Germans much.

We were to start twenty minutes later, and I remember thinking that that twenty minutes would just be time enough for the Germans to wake up and put down their counter barrage.

But things happened very similarly to the 31st July, 1917, and we got on the way unmolested. The fog was very trying, and one could only see a few yards. Our route lay past the old aerodrome which had been just behind our old front line, and on along a road and through the old trenches, and thence across country to a well-known feature of the country known as the "Tree and a half," it being an isolated tree and the remains of another, and which on a clear day was visible for a very long way; this feature had been drummed into us since the attack was mooted, and it was not thought possible for us to lose our way.

But the trouble was we couldn't see anything; the situation was wrapped in mystery. We got to the old German second line, a rambling trench, crossed it, got hung up in the wire, recrossed it again unwittingly, and then started wondering where we were. I once more had that lost sensation as on the Bronbeck; once more I tried to distinguish between the noise made by our guns and theirs; once again got it wrong. Meanwhile, shells started arriving amongst us; the adjutant, Alec Agar-Robartes, had been following me up, and I held consultation with him; it was then we remembered that interesting, but usually much despised article of equipment, the compass. We knew we ought to be going pretty well due south, but our compasses indicated that we were heading for home, so we turned about with eye glued to the compass, at last saw the Tree and a half, and took up our position in reserve according to plan; this was just south-west of the village of Moyenneville.

We had no inkling of how the other companies were faring; the battlefield seemed strangely deserted, and one wondered what had happened and where it had happened.

The commanding officer, Colonel Thorne, had gone on ahead of the reserve company to direct the front wave; he was second to none on an occasion of this sort; the fog had no terrors for him, and he always knew exactly where he was on the map; we were fortunate indeed to have him leading us, as he converted what looked like a ghastly muddle into a brilliant success. Shortly after our arrival at our objective, he appeared from the front after having located the support company in front, but having seen nothing of Nos. 3 and 4. Directly after, Tufnell and

Hirst, commanding these companies, came up and reported that they too had been lost in the fog, and were now behind us in an old German trench.

Thus, as Nos. 2 and 1 Companies were now in front, it was decided on a change of plan. I was ordered to take my company forward and make good a road some 400 yards in front; so we went on through the fog. Just before we started, a company of Scots Guards, lost like the rest of us, appeared from the German lines led by a tank, and were about to attack us, thinking we were Germans; we stopped this in time, and it was arranged that they should dig in on our left.

Our job wasn't thought too pleasant, as there were machine guns barking, and none too far away; but we made good our road without much trouble, except for a few shells. I returned to B.H.Q. as ordered, and reported my new position; a conference before this was perhaps one of the most remarkable councils of war ever held; it consisted of the C.O., the adjutant, the intelligence officer, three company commanders and a tank officer, and we all sat in one shell hole with German shells bursting all round, poring over maps and trying to look and feel unconcerned. The C.O. gave his orders as clearly and concisely as if sitting in the orderly room at home, and we, seeing him, daren't be frightened, and I remember my greatest anxiety being that I should not be able to produce the correct trench map, or find my place on it when produced. Such is the power of discipline, which, whatever anyone may say, is the finest thing in the world, enabling men to do things they couldn't possibly do without it.

Well, on reporting again to the C.O., who had by now got the situation well in hand, I was ordered to carry on the advance and capture the objective originally allotted to No. 3 Company. No. 2 Company would conform, and capture No. 4 Company's objective.

So I returned to the company, and got them formed up in two lines, Nos. 1 and 2 platoons in front, under Delacombe, followed closely by 3 and 4, under Clough Taylor; the fog was now lifting somewhat, and the sun showed vaguely; the sun was pretty well the line of our advance, and I ordered the men to march on the sun, and so once again the heavens came to our rescue. It seemed a long way; half-way there we ran into a battalion of Royal Scots, and I had a short talk about the situation with their C.O. before going on; he told me what he knew of the situation, and I gathered that a battalion of the Shropshire Light Infantry were ahead of them, and had reached the railway line.

After leaving them, we had to go over a ridge with our railway in the shallow valley below; this meant advancing down a sort of glacis, and now the fog had lifted, in full view of the enemy; it was not pleasant, and machine gun bullets zipped past us, and I don't know why we weren't all killed. Anyhow, by short bursts of doubling we reached the shelter of the railway embankment; there we found the Shropshires and, to our surprise, half a platoon of our No. 3 Company, under Duff Cooper; they had done most gallantly, and carrying out their instructions to reach their objective at all costs, had arrived there and were waiting developments; they couldn't tell us much about the situation, except that the enemy was in strength on the far side of the embankment. which they were raking with M.G. fire, and that they believed No. 2 Company was on their left, but did not know their exact position; so I put my company, or two platoons of it, in on their left, the other two platoons remaining in the shelter of the valley behind.

We then decided to go and look for No. 2 Company, the party being Cooper, my C.S.M. (Marks), a runner, and myself; we continued along the embankment until the line became level; then there was a thin hedge, and we heard a machine gun firing from it; here, we thought, is No. 2 Company—all is well; but on getting closer we noticed the barrel pointing towards our lines, and a section of fat grey figures crouching round it. Well, this looked too good a bag to miss, and they hadn't seen us; so we turned back and organised a small attack; I detailed Cooper and his men to creep up and rush the post, with my No. 1 platoon following up to help if necessary, and to consolidate the ground gained. This operation was most successful, though we had a few men hit; the German machine gunners, eighteen of them, surrendered *en bloc*, and we dug in along the hedge.

I next discovered No. 2 Company a little bit back behind a bank; they had been led most gallantly by Allan Adair, and had done their job well. Their bank was under heavy machine gun fire from some way back, and it was not deemed advisable for the moment for him to advance his men up to my left. The Germans started now firing field guns practically over open sights at us, and we weren't having too good a time; not long after the machine gun fire relaxed a bit, and No. 2 Company was able to reach the railway, which opposite them ran through a cutting; during this operation many prisoners were taken, machine gunners who had either got tired of firing, or who had fired their last shot and had retired to temporary safety in dugouts; they surrendered tamely enough.

Thus, our line was established, and the Coldstream having been located on our left, our flanks were secured, and we set to work to consolidate our new position.

We dug ourselves well in all along the railway, with supports close behind. There was a small quarry nearby with a respectable dugout in it, and this I fixed as my C.H.Q., inviting Allan Adair to join me there, which he did. There was a lot of shelling of the embankment the rest of that day, but our quarry was left pretty much alone. It was risky work going round the line, as enemy machine gunners used to take shots at one walking along.

At night we pushed posts forward into some old German rifle pits; I sent one of my support platoons out in front, under Sergeant Habberjam.

That night passed off fairly uneventfully; we were content with our day's work, the commanding officer had praised us, and we heard that the higher authorities were well pleased, and so we were contented. It is hardly necessary to say the men were wonderful—they always were. Were it possible to mention them all by name in this book I would do so, but as it isn't, I mention instead their officers as representing them. No one was more loyally served by the men under him than I was, from the

114

C.S.M. to the youngest guardsman; and we, as officers, indeed had our way made smooth by having such magnificent men to command. The most difficult job a company commander had was to select names to recommend for decorations; all deserved them, whereas only four or five got them after each show.

But to return to the battle. On the morning of the 22nd at dawn we were just getting ready to stand to arms in the ordinary way when the Germans opened a terrific barrage on us, and a messenger arrived from the front line to say the Germans were coming over; we raced out from our quarry, ran the gauntlet of innumerable shells, and reached the railway safely; the situation was a bit obscure; one could see nothing from our part of the line, though No. 2 Company, lower down, reported seeing enemy advancing.

Someone on our right sent up the S.O.S., our artillery put down a very good and accurate barrage, and all was quiet; it was impossible to get communication with our front platoon during this time, and we had no idea how they were faring. One German in full marching order came over to our lines and gave himself up; it transpired later that it was an organised counter-attack with the idea of regaining all they had lost the day before. It failed completely, and the attacking Germans were pinned to their ground and remained in the various trenches and shell holes where they had been brought to a standstill.

When things quietened a bit, an attempt was made to get communication with the front platoon, and to send them up more ammunition. Delacombe, who was company patrol officer, attempted to crawl up with two men, but both men were hit, and it was with difficulty that he got back all right. It didn't seem possible to get up there, but Delacombe was not to be beaten, and he volunteered to try again by a different way, making use of some old horse standings in front of our line as cover; this time he succeeded, and brought back most useful information; the garrison in front were all right; they kept out the enemy in spite of great pressure, and had behaved most gallantly; Sergeant Habberjam was recommended by the platoon for the D.C.M., which he got; it was a fine performance.

The rest of that day was very trying; we were all tired, and the Germans shelled us relentlessly all day, and also trench-mortared us; they got on to our quarry, and it became far from healthy.

We had several visitors from the outside world, all full of congratulations, among them Head, the senior chaplain, whose presence in dangerous times was always an inspiration; I doubt if I ever met a calmer man at such times, or one who had himself so completely under control.

There were rumours of our being relieved that night, and later a definite message came to this effect. Later this was cancelled, and an inter-company relief was arranged instead; we were to be relieved by No. 3 Company, and go back to a bank a little way back; No. 3 had been shelled heavily all day too, and I don't think we should have gained much by the exchange, apart from being relieved of the responsibility of holding the front line, and the front platoon required relaxation, however small.

I had handed the whole thing over to Tufnell, and showed him all our depositions, when another message arrived cancelling the company relief, and telling us to send to B.H.Q. for several yards of white tape. Well, this looked like a night attack, it being the custom to wear white tape on one's arms to distinguish friend from foe. It transpired that the attack was to be pushed next day, and we were to attack again and take a strong enemy trench some 500 yards on, known as Hammoville Trench; Nos. 3 and 4 Companies were to do the actual attack, No. 2 was to support; we, No. 1, were to withdraw from our advanced positions during our barrage, and reoccupy them twenty minutes after zero hour, and also a line of pits a little further on, thence we were to be in reserve to help if required. The attack was timed for 3 a.m.

We had previously had a conference in our little dugout in the quarry, the C.O., company commanders, and all the platoon commanders, and huddled up there together we made our plans; time was short, and we only just had time enough to get things ready by 3 a.m. My dispositions were as follows: My No.

3 platoon, which had been in front, was to remain in the embankment with C.H.Q., the other three platoons were to move forward at 3.20 to the allotted objectives in front. At 3 a.m. I was in C.H.Q., a deepish dugout, very narrow and dark; our barrage opened with terrific force; the Germans opened one simultaneously, apparently also intending to attack. At 3.20 I had to get out of my more or less safe refuge to see the other three platoons to their destination, and I had arranged to go with two runners, leaving the rest of my headquarters behind.

It was awful waiting for those twenty minutes to pass; a veritable hail of shells outside, all sizes up to 8-inch, and knowing that I had to go out and face the storm, it was a terrible temptation to stay in the dugout and run the show from there, but, thank God, I didn't, and I went out with my two runners; crossing the railway a shell came very close, and we lay down to avoid the shock; after the earth stopped falling I told them to get up, but one of them (Jones) never moved again; he was just by my side, and had been killed by the shock. It was a wonderful sight out there, still dark, and a red wave of shells going on ahead; the men went well; some of my company went on with the first wave in their enthusiasm.

The attack was a tremendous success; our companies were very weak, but the Germans were taken quite by surprise, and surrendered wholesale; the earth seemed to open and give up Germans; the front companies captured many times their own number. The enemy kept up a heavy fire on the railway for some time, and when it got. light things quietened down. And then followed one of the most interesting days I spent in the whole war. The 1st Battalion Coldstream came through us, and attacked up to Judas Farm, near Ervillers, and later our 1st Battalion came through in perfect formation and attacked the Mory Switch trench; there was no more wonderful sight than watching that battalion go up in artillery formation, and then deploy and attack; later still, gunners galloped up and actually went in front of where we started the day, and we really began to think things were getting a move on.

Delacombe was wounded early in the day and Carstairs

joined the company.

That night the 2nd Battalion Scots Guards relieved us, and we marched back dead tired, but full of the joy of victory, to Ayette, where we lived in the old trenches there. We thought we had got away from the war, but to our disgust a heavy naval gun started shelling Ayette next morning, and kept it up at intervals all day. This was more than we could stand, and we were ordered further back to old gun positions behind Adinfer Wood, where we lived in peace and refitted, and got ready for the next battle.

About this time Colonel Thorne left us, to our general regret, to command first an army school, and then a brigade; Lord Lascelles took over command, and later Major Pearson Gregory came as second in command.

CHAPTER 23

The 1918 Offensive: (2) Canal du Nord

I was left out of the next battle, and Elliott took my company in. As far as possible those who had been in the previous battle were left out of this one. I therefore went back to Berles au Bois, where our details had moved to.

The new offensive started on September 2nd, but the battalion was not engaged till the next day. They had a long and rather trying march up, and had to go through all the usual anxieties, but the attack itself turned out to be a walk over; the usual barrage was put down, but the enemy had cleared from his position.

The battalion started from the Vaulx Vraucourt area, and advanced through Lagnicourt and Boursies, and the enemy was finally bumped into his old Hindenburg Line about the Canal du Nord.

There were very few casualties in the attack, but while digging in later the right half battalion were very heavily gassed, and lost all their six officers and a large proportion of the men. Thus Elliott, Inglis Jones and Calvocoressi of No. 1 Company, and Dury, Henderson and Manley of No. 2 Company, were gassed, and did not return to the battalion.

The details were sent for as reinforcements, and we also had a draft from the 4th Battalion, which had been withdrawn from the firing line after their experiences at Nieppe Forest, and were now at Le Treport on the sea.

We rejoined the battalion on the 9th; I found a very attenuated company, only about twenty-five men left under a corporal. The reinforcements only brought us up to a little over fifty, so for some time we were very weak, and there was a good deal of reorganising to do. Luckily my C.S.M. had been left out of the fight, and he, together with the C.Q.M.S. (Dore) were of the greatest assistance in pulling the company together again.

The battalion was in reserve west of Lagnicourt till the 15th, and we put in a good deal of training and recreation before moving further forward east of Lagnicourt and west of Doignies and Louverval.

Allan Adair got command of No. 2 Company, vice Dury, and I had Carstairs and Donnison in No. 1, Clough Taylor having gone temporarily to the brigade as gas officer.

Things meanwhile were pretty lively on the Canal du Nord; the trenches west of it were still held in places by the Germans, and it was deemed advisable to make good all the ground up to the actual canal before the next advance was started.

On our particular front this was done in places, but not altogether; on our right the canal swung back, and the next division were dug in on the east side; away on our left at Moeuvres there was continuous and confused fighting, the village changing hands about twice daily.

Bourlon Wood was the dominating feature of this country; it was still in German hands, and seemed to look down on us wherever we went; thus by day we were pretty well overlooked.

There was a new attack in preparation, though the exact date was not known. It was to be one of the biggest of the series, and aimed at the capture of the formidable Hindenburg defences, and the driving of the enemy into more or less open country. The job of the battalion was to clean up the trenches west of the canal, while the Scots Guards on our right crossed the canal and similarly the Coldstream on the left. We were given the lightest job, as we had to hold the front line previous to the attack.

I will explain this attack later, as we had a tour of duty in the

120

trenches first which was not altogether devoid of interest.

We went into the line on the 23rd; my company was on the extreme right of the brigade's front and next to the Royal Scots of the 3rd Division; our line ran up to the canal, and the Germans had posts just on the far side.

It had been fairly lively there, and the 3rd Division had been attacked a few days before; the attack was beaten off, and the 1st Battalion Coldstream, who were holding the line on their left, had a wonderful enfilade shoot, and wrought great slaughter on the attackers.

We relieved the Welsh Guards here; there were some wonderful dugouts here, twenty or thirty feet deep, where one could get away from the war and have a sleep when not on duty, so we weren't too badly off. We got in for a bad barrage on the morning of the 25th. half-an-hour of the best, and it looked as if the enemy was going to attack; it was very severe while it lasted, and we stood to arms dodging the shells as best we might. Nothing else happened to us, but it was thought that an attempt was made to raid posts held by our No. 3 Company; the attempt was half-hearted, and resulted in nothing. We had a few casualties, but nothing very alarming.

We were busy all this time getting ready for the great offensive, which we now learnt was fixed for the early morning of the 27th. If successful, this battle was to have far-reaching effects; it was ambitious, the Hindenburg Line being by no means a light proposition. It turned out to be one of the most successful days of this type of close fighting experienced during the war; it may well be called the beginning of the end; from thence onward things went with a rush, the enemy's morale was finished, and the war collapsed with startling suddenness.

But to return to the actual battle; as I said before, our task was comparatively light. No. 3 Company, under de Geijer, was to do the actual attack, supported by No. 4, under Bunbury; while No. 2, under Adair, held their original position on the left. My company was to be in Brigade Reserve, and for that purpose was to be withdrawn to the dugouts in which B.H.Q. had lived, and there to await developments.

On the night of the 26th, the 1st Batt. Scots Guards relieved my company and took over their battle positions; they were pretty well squashed up in their trenches, each of my platoons being relieved by a company, but their job was severe, and it was necessary for them to attack in strength; the canal, although empty, was broad and with steep sides; portable scaling ladders were used.

On relief we went back to the trenches known as Walsh Support, and were secreted in dugouts there. Personally I did not expect we should have anything to do next day, as the attack was on a big scale, and the 1st and 3rd Guards' Brigades were to go through the 2nd, and finally the 2nd Division were in reserve to go through further.

Our division was now commanded by Major-General Matheson, who succeeded General Feilding, who left to command the London district.

The attack started a trifle before dawn; it had rained during the night, and the assembled troops had rather a poor time, added to this the Germans started shelling heavily just before our attack was due to start.

We put down probably the heaviest barrage of the war, and the attack everywhere met with success, except that on our left, in the next division's area who were to attack in flank that section of the Hindenburg Line between us and Moeuvres, there were some trenches uncleared, and the machine gunners in these proved very tough fighters, and gave a lot of trouble to the 1st Battalion Coldstream, and also at longer range to our front companies, who, by the way, had accomplished their task perfectly, with very few casualties, and taking several prisoners.

So it was that, although the attack had gone on well beyond the canal, and on towards Rumilly, which was the farthest point it was hoped to reach, there were still those men on our flank holding out; they were, of course, surrounded, and never had any hope of escape; but it so happened that their regimental commander was going his rounds when the attack started, and he, no doubt, was the cause of their not surrendering long before. As a result of this, the Coldstream, although they had captured their own objective all right, were having difficulty in consolidating.

In the afternoon I was ordered to take my company up to the canal to support the Coldstream, who were organising a bombing attack to deal with these people. So we marched off there, thinking that, after all, we were going to have a show. But just as we got up, we saw a wonderful sight—swarms of people advancing to our flank, preceded by a tank; they were the next door division, who should have arrived at 9 a.m.; when they did arrive, they did their job well, and the tank soon persuaded the Germans that their game was up, and out they came, some 200 of them, headed by the afore-mentioned regimental commander, as dapper a little man as I have ever seen, perfectly dressed, with a spotless, tight-fitting grey overcoat, kid gloves, an ebony walking stick and a large cigar. He seemed to take his fate very philosophically, no doubt pleased at having put up so good a fight.

Well, after this there was nothing else for us to do, so we returned once more to Walsh Support.

It had been an interesting day; the attack had gone well all along the line, and at the end of the day the line ran just west of the Canal de l'Escaut in the Marcoing district. The Canadians, on the left, had taken Bourlon Wood, and advanced well beyond it. The enemy still had strong trenches about Marcoing and Masnières, but his main defences had gone, and he must have been in a pretty bad way.

That night we went back to Doignies to bivouac.

It was a great advantage being the first troops in the attack, as, all being well, one got a rest the same night, instead of having the additional fatigue of holding the ground gained.

We had about ten days at Doignies, resting and training, and we were quite happy there.

A few more officers arrived, notably Eric Anson, who had been out twice before, and K. A. Campbell, who came to No. 1 Company as my second in command; he had been previously with some Yeomanry, and later the Household Battalion; Gunther was also posted to the company, vice Donnison, who went to No. 4 Company.

In the beginning of September, Agar-Robartes, the adjutant, went on the staff, and his place was taken by Fitzgerald, Cornish becoming assistant adjutant.

CHAPTER 24,

The 1918 Offensive:
Estourmel to Maubeuge

On the evening of the 7th October we left Doignies and marched up to bivouac just west of Marcoing, to be in reserve to the 2nd Division, who were attacking next morning.

During our stay at Doignies, the 2nd and 3rd Divisions had pushed on and established themselves east of Rumilly; on the 8th they were to push on again, and the 2nd Division, which concerned us, was to capture a strongish trench, and also the small village of Forenville, and we were to go through them.

We had an uncomfortable night on the 7th-8th; we had some difficulty in finding our bivouacs, owing to our guides losing their way in the dark, which was not to be wondered at really, as in this devastated country there were practically no landmarks. So we arrived very late at night, and had to settle ourselves in in the dark, and it was none too warm; personally, I didn't get too much sleep that night; the German naval gunners were pretty active, too, and remained so all that night and most of the next day.

If the attack was very successful on the 8th, it was likely that we should go through the same day, but ordinarily we weren't to take the field till the 9th; our immediate objective was to take a high railway embankment east of Forenville, but we were also allotted various tentative objectives further on in the event of things going unexpectedly well.

My company was to be on the right, in front, with No. 2 under Adair on my left, with No. 4 in support under Bunbury, and No. 3 under Anson in reserve.

About midday on the 8th we had orders to move up across the Canal de l'Escaut to the Masnières area; the 2nd Division had got on fairly well, but had not quite reached their final objective; they had incidentally been counter-attacked by tanks, and the Germans seemed to be showing some fight.

We remained in trenches round Masnières till late at night on the 8th-9th; we had sent up parties to reconnoitre our assembly positions east of Rumilly, and spent the rest of the day studying the map, and wondering what the morrow had in store for us.

We got mildly gas shelled on the way, and there was a horrible smell of stale gas about the streets of Rumilly, but it was not necessary to put on gas helmets; we found our assembly positions all right; the plan was for the 2nd Division to go back to rest as soon as we got into position.

Our attack was to start at dawn; we had our 2nd Battalion on our right.

That night was, in many ways, a remarkable one; Cambrai was just on our left, and was burning fiercely all night, and was, as far as we could see, being shelled by both sides; it was a tragic sight, and impressed us a good deal. In the middle of the night fresh and final orders arrived, necessitating conferences in the dark; there were a few minor alterations in the plans, including a preliminary advance before zero. However, everything was ready well before the starting time.

The night had been disturbed up till about, midnight, when the Germans suddenly became dead quiet; not a shell or a bullet came our way. I began to wonder if he had cleared off again, but daren't suggest the idea, lest it should bring down a shower of shells on to us.

At the appointed hour our barrage came down, and we advanced; no opposition, no trouble at all, except for some of our own guns firing short; it seemed such a pity one couldn't switch off the barrage and just advance without it, but it was not possible. We saw our railway embankment, and could have got to it long before, but our barrage necessitated our going slow; I had expected this embankment would have given us a lot of trouble; I had pictured masses of machine guns firing from the top of it, and another day such as August 21st. But there wasn't a soul there, and as soon as our guns ceased firing on it, we took possession and had some breakfast.

Having achieved our actual final objective without opposition, it was obvious we should have to follow up to our tentative objectives—Wambaix Copse, Estourmel, and the Cambrai-Le Cateau road. We couldn't tell then, how far the enemy had gone back; it had been foreshadowed that he meant that his next real line of resistance to be the line of the River Selle about Solesmes; so it occurred to us that he might have already gone right back there, and I remember the commanding officer optimistically saying that we could treat the rest of the day as a "scheme."

But, although undoubtedly his main body had gone right back, yet strong rearguards with plentiful artillery remained to bar our path. Our method of advancing was to be cautious, and strong patrols were to precede us and report all clear before a general advance. Thus, patrols were sent out to Wambaix Copse, a small wood half a mile on, and on its being reported clear, the companies advanced; these patrols consisted of one platoon under an officer; Gunther had charge of my patrol.

Next, the village of Estourmel had to be investigated; the same patrol went on while we pushed on over the open country, and waited just outside the village; the 2nd Battalion, on our right, co-operated with us.

On the patrol entering the village the enemy made his first signs of life, and started shelling the eastern approaches with field guns; nothing heavy, and probably not more than one battery was in action, but it was enough to tell us we were not to have everything our own way. The patrol gained the village all right, and took a few prisoners from the cellars; they established themselves in a sunken road on the far side, and sent back a message to us to come on.

Meanwhile, the shelling was getting more severe, and a machine gun started; we had to cross over a ridge, and on reaching the top were heavily fired on by machine guns; we deployed and doubled into the valley below; there was yet another ridge to cross before reaching the sunken road; my plan was to reach the objective from the south side of the village, and skirting it, as it was now under heavy shell fire; the difficulty now was to get over the next ridge without having casualties.

I left the company in the valley, and went on with Campbell and a runner to see how the land lay; to our great joy we found another sunken road which led right into our objective, and thus it was possible to get there without crossing the ridge, and quite unseen. The 2nd Battalion, on our right, had no such luck, and were pretty well pinned to their ground about the village of Cattenières. Two platoons managed to get forward, and came in on my right in the sunken road.

We discovered that the machine gun fire came from an isolated factory called Bolstrancourt; it was surrounded with trees and a hedge, and there were also some trenches there. This factory dominated our position entirely, and as we had got right away, now, from our artillery, the idea of further advance was abandoned for the moment. The shelling became very severe, and a German aeroplane came over just above our heads, and must have located us exactly.

We began having casualties, and our easy day turned after all into rather a strenuous one.

I had three platoons in the sunken road, with the fourth dug in, in a ploughed field to connect up with No. 2 Company, who were in another sunken road, with troops forward in some buildings known as Igniel dit les Frisettes; these latter were on the Cambrai–Le Cateau road, and were so heavily shelled that they had to be evacuated, and the men dug in behind.

The shelling was continuous all that day, especially in the villages of Estourmel and Cattenières. Our guns could not get forward to help us, so it was rather one-sided.

That night I was ordered to push forward under cover of

darkness to the main road, and dig in beyond it; the 2nd Battalion were to advance, and rush Bolstrancourt, and connect up with us. This operation was carried out successfully, and without opposition, and the enemy was on the move again, and at midnight his guns stopped firing. Our advance was to be continued in the morning.

The 1st Battalion Scots Guards were to go through us, and advance, if possible, to St. Hilaire, through Carnières and Boussières. We were to follow them up.

It was a much more interesting form of war than we had grown accustomed to; practically the open warfare we had sighed for for years.

We advanced on the 10th, with no artillery support; the battalion advanced along the road by platoons; Nos. 3 and 4 Companies led, with No. 1 next, and No. 2 behind. cavalry patrols made their appearance, and it was all very interesting. We halted first at an isolated farm-house just west of Carnières, and then went on through Carnières to the high ground beyond; here we once more came under shell fire, and they put a salvo at my company H.Q., which I had established in a cottage.

Things seemed to be going well in front, and we just had time to snatch a very hurried lunch before being ordered on again, this time through Boussières; we encountered fairly heavy field gun fire on the way, but got to the far side of the village all right, and dug in along a bank. That was as far as we got that day, as the Scots Guards bumped the enemy in front of St. Hilaire, and were held up.

We made ourselves as comfortable as we could; there was a good deal of shelling, but it was wild and inaccurate, and didn't really worry us very much.

Next day the 3rd Guards' Brigade took up the chase, and their objective was to capture Solesmes, if possible, and then exploit their success. We were to march to St. Vaast, a village just east of St. Hilaire, and billet there; both these places were in German hands still. Some of our guns had by now moved forward, so we again had support.

We didn't actually move till about 9 a.m. on the 11th, to give the 3rd Brigade time to get forward. As it happened, they found things a bit more difficult than was expected, and they were held up on the far side of St. Vaast. This was the limit of the advance that day. Our experience was rather odd; we marched up in fours to St. Hilaire, along roads crowded with transport, to find the enemy only just out of the town, and machine gun bullets flying over the houses. So we halted in St. Hilaire, and were put into billets there. We found a very comfortable house to live in, but I felt all the time we were in a fool's paradise; the enemy were only a few hundred yards away; if you put your head outside the door a bullet would swish past it. It seemed all wrong being so comfortable so close up; I felt also that the house was probably mined, and might go up in the air any moment.

The Germans had done a lot of mining; there were continually large explosions going on; also booby traps were plentiful; an expert sapper used to go round the billets looking for bombs under the pianos, or traps concealed in the rooms. We luckily never got caught by one of these.

As it turned out, we had a very peaceful day at St. Hilaire, and next day a battalion dinner was arranged in one of the best houses in the place, and a truly remarkable meal resulted, and eaten amongst every sign of luxury and well-being. I well remember the look of surprise and incredulity on the face of a sapper officer on his way from the front line, who came to ask his way.

The Germans gradually completed their withdrawal to the river Selle; this left rather a curious position, as the river ran through the village of St. Python, thus giving us half the town and them the other half, with civilians living in both halves.

We relieved the 2nd Battalion Scots Guards there on the 13th. They had had rather a bad time there, and the position in the village was a bit tricky. No. 4 Company, under Bunbury, held the actual village, my company was behind in trenches, and I had my H.Q. in an isolated house with a big but unsafe cellar.

No. 4 had a very curious experience in St. Python. The inhabitants used to come and fall on their necks, and give them coffee and eggs, and the company lived on the fat of the land; but all the time there were snipers across the stream, and civilians, as well as soldiers, were killed and wounded. They had their H.Q. in a house in the village, very pleasant and comfortable inside, but it was death to walk into the street by day.

We, further back, were doing just ordinary trench work. Shells were plentiful, and every morning early we were gassed, chiefly with the sneezing variety, which was most unpleasant. Our little house had many narrow escapes from being hit; the people who relieved us abandoned it as unsafe, a shell having landed on the doorstep.

The Germans were in strength here, and commanded us with the high ground east of Solesmes, and their gunners gave us little peace.

Before a further advance, it was necessary to arrange a big barrage, and also the stream required bridging.

Several attempts were made to get a footing on the far side; the Coldstream and Scots Guards both sent companies across, but they got cut off, and were only extricated with the greatest difficulty. We had men across at one time, but later relied on patrols for keeping the far bank clear.

On the 16th the 24th Division on our left attacked and temporarily captured the village of Haussy; they were forced back by a counter-attack later in the day.

Meanwhile, the Guards' Division's attack was getting ready; it was to be carried out by the 1st and 3rd Guards' Brigades, and we were to be in reserve at St. Vaast. The object of the attack was to capture Solesmes and the high ground beyond.

We were relieved by the 1st Battalion Scots Guards on the 17th, and returned to St. Vaast.

St. Vaast got shelled a good deal, and it was no health resort at that time; however, we were comfortably billeted.

On the 20th the attack took place, and was a complete success, and the 2nd Guards' Brigade was not called for.

On the 22nd the 2nd Division relieved us, and so our fortnight's continuous fighting came to an end; it was perhaps the most strenuous and interesting time of the whole war. The battalion marched back to Boussières to rest; on the way back, a few high shrapnel shells burst over us, and they were the last shells I ever saw burst.

On the 24th I went on leave, returning on November 7th, to be greeted at Boulogne with the news that the war was over; the town was much excited, but it turned out they were premature rejoicings, and the news was false.

During my absence the battalion took part in its last battle, on November 4th, when they captured Preux au Sart after one of the stiffest and most difficult fights of the war. Campbell took in my company, and most gallantly he led them; they suffered very heavy casualties, Campbell and Carstairs were wounded, and Gunther killed while attending to the latter's wounds.

Geoffrey Gunther was a great loss; he was a boy of exceptional promise and charm, and it was cruel luck his being killed in the last battle of the war.

The battalion followed up their advance, and finally had the crowning success of taking Maubeuge, being the first troops into the town; they were received with unbounded enthusiasm by the inhabitants.

I rejoined the details at Carnières, and remained there till the 12th, when we all went up to Maubeuge. We celebrated Armistice quietly at Carnières; there was not much means of doing anything else. The massed drums of the division played in the square, but that was about all that happened.

CHAPTER 25

The March to Germany

It was difficult to realise that the war was over, and that after all one wasn't going to be killed as one had expected. And yet there wasn't really very much excitement among the troops; we had got so into the habit of taking everything for granted, and we took the end of the war as quietly as we had the beginning; in both instances we felt a sense of satisfaction.

I rejoined the battalion on the 12th at Maubeuge; we were billeted right in the city, and quite well off there. I found my company much reduced in strength, and temporarily commanded by Eric Anson. On my return, he went back to No. 3, and I had Chetwynd Stapylton, who had just come out, and Clough Taylor under me.

Maubeuge was pretty well intact, except for nearly all the bridges over the Sambre, which were destroyed. The inhabitants were most genial, and delighted at their changed circumstances. The mayor, after an impressive service in the cathedral and a further ceremony in the square, presented the major-general (General Matheson) with a flag to commemorate the retaking of the city; the greatest enthusiasm prevailed.

According to the Armistice terms we were to allow the enemy a week's start before following him up, so we stayed at Maubeuge till the 18th, when we moved on to Rouveroy, thence next day at Mont St. Genevieve.

We received a very cordial welcome at both these villages, which were decorated in our honour with flags and triumphal arches everywhere. But our greatest welcome was to be next day, the 20th, when we entered Charleroi; perhaps the greatest pitch of enthusiasm was reached at Marchiennes au Pont, a suburb of Charleroi; here the crowds were particularly dense and enthusiastic; the town band of top-hatted citizens turned out to greet us. Charleroi was packed with people, crowds at every window, as well as in the streets, and it was a wonderful sight, and one never to be forgotten.

We had magnificent billets there, and the men were in the barracks; we only had three nights there. At night everyone was in the streets; dense crowds in the square listening to the Coldstream band playing; the whole town was lit up, and altogether gave itself up to rejoicing; we gave a dinner to the people who billeted us, at the best restaurant in the place, preceded by a small dance.

On the 24th we left for Presles, on the 25th for Lesves, where we stayed three nights, and thence on to Maillen, where we stayed a week.

Our march was one long triumphal progress, and was most interesting, and the country was charming.

At Maillen we had to wait for our food supplies to catch us up. I paid a visit to Namur from there one day. Our next move was to Havelange on the 5th December, Barvaux on the 6th, and Werbomont on the 7th. There we stayed three days, moving thence to Wanne, which was only a few miles from the frontier. Wild boar hunts used to be arranged during our halts, and the boars killed made a welcome addition to the men's daily stew.

On the 12th the "Great Day" arrived, and we marched into Germany. It rained, of course, but that did not damp our ardour, and we marched into the enemy's country to the strains of the "British Grenadiers," the corps commander (General Haldane) taking the salute on the border.

The character of our march now changed; instead of the hilarious greetings we had had up to now, we were received in silence, but not indifference; crowds collected as before, but they just stared vacantly, except the children, who loved the drums and marched along beside them.

Our first billet was at Deidenburg; the inhabitants were quite civil, and did not seem to mind us being there very much. On the 13th we left for Nidrum.

Our destination was to be Düren, and we were to march the whole way. But plans were suddenly altered, owing chiefly, I think, to the civil troubles in Cologne.

Thus the 2nd Guards' Brigade were ordered on by train to Cologne on the 14th (the 2nd Battalion Irish Guards rejoined us at Maubeuge, so we were a full brigade again). The remainder of the division were to continue the journey by road, so we were in luck's way.

We reached Cologne that evening about 10 p.m., and marched triumphantly through the town to the infantry barracks at Riehl; the drums played appropriately "When we wind up the Watch on the Rhine" on our leaving the station; it pleased us very much, but I am afraid it was lost on the Germans.

CHAPTER 26

Cologne: and Home Again

I do not intend to write much about our life in Cologne; it was very much like garrison duty anywhere else.

We were very comfortable; the civilians were civil, even cringing; we had no trouble from anyone; our methods were firm; salutes were required from anyone in uniform, and civilians, if spoken to, had to remove their hats. When we were on the march anyone failing to comply with these rules was immediately arrested and taken for a walk; there was a pretty liberal interpretation of what a uniform was, and several inoffensive members of the Cologne Yachting Club were arrested, their peaked caps being sufficiently like uniform for us!, I remember one luckless postman in the act of delivering letters being marched off miles from his beat. We enjoyed the game immensely, and it showed the Germans we meant business.

On the 16th I was in charge of a Guard of Honour for the commander-in-chief; it was many a day since we had done anything of this sort, and I confess to having been very near a ceremonial disaster at one time!

Our daily work consisted of drill or a route march; the men had splendid barracks with a colossal square. They played a lot of football, and we did what we could to find amusements for them. In the town there was the opera, various cabarets where one sat and drank light wine, and listened to a show, and later on English pierrot shows and pantomimes arrived.

We were on guard three days out of every nine; there were

various guards, on all the Headquarters and all the bridges. It took practically the whole battalion to find these, and it made a change from the usual routine. We used to go on guard as much like King's Guard as we could, and tried to impress the inhabitants; I don't know if we did, but there was always a crowd to watch guard mountings.

We had quite a cheerful Christmas, and on the 28th demobilisation commenced; it only reached a certain point, as we found we were getting too weak in numbers; but anyhow we said goodbye to a good many old trusted warriors.

Patrick Ellison and Ivo Grenfell joined the company in Cologne, and later Martin; and Campbell returned, recovered from his wound.

On January 7th the colours arrived from England, and were received with due ceremony, reminding the Germans, as they said, of the days of their former greatness.

Only twice was there any trouble; once when a strike threatened, and the other time during the elections; in neither case did anything occur.

The weather was very cold for a spell in January and February, and skating became general. We had one man drowned trying to save a German who had fallen in; I think they were genuinely touched by this, and sent a representative to the funeral.

In the middle of February the 4th Battalion was broken up, together with the 2nd Battalion Irish Guards, and the 4th Battalion Coldstream; thus we received considerable reinforcement.

It was said, more or less definitely, that we were to be out there a year or more. But this too was altered, and on the 27th February we left *en route* for England.

Our joy was great.

We stayed three nights at Dunkirk, sailing on March 4th for Tilbury, arriving next morning. So our long stay abroad had finished, and we were really home for good.

It was raining when we got to London, but all the same we got the welcome home which we had looked forward to for years; and the band played "See the Conquering Hero Comes" as we got out of the train; and with uncased colours and fixed bayonets, we marched through the city to the Tower of London, which was to be our new quarters.

And so the end came, and with it a feeling of intense thankfulness and relief.

Lightning Source UK Ltd.
Milton Keynes UK
UKOW040712030513

210162UK00001B/99/P